FOURTEENTH ANNUAL

100 SHOW American Center for Design

DESIGN YEAR IN REVIEW

1992 : **American Center for Design** is a member-based organization of design professionals, educators and students. In addition to promoting excellence in design education and practice, it serves as a national center for the accumulation and dissemination of information regarding design and its role in our culture and economy.

© 1992 American Center for Design

Published in Chicago by the American Center for Design, 233 East Ontario Street, Chicago, Illinois 60611. Distributed to the trade by Watson-Guptill Publications, 1515 Broadway, New York, New York 10036. Distributed outside the US and Canada by RotoVision SA, 9, route Suisse, CH-1295 Mies, Switzerland. Telephone : (022) 755 30 55, Fax : (022) 755 40 72.

ISBN 0-8230-6176-0

PRINTED IN THE USA BY TOTAL REPRODUCTIONS, INC. BOOK DESIGN: KATHERINE McCOY, TIMOTHY O'KEEFFE AND MARK D SYLVESTER AT THE CRANBROOK ACADEMY OF ART, BLOOMFIELD HILLS, MICHIGAN EDITOR: ROB DEWEY

For information about membership in the American Center for Design, contact: American Center for Design, 233 East Ontario Street, Chicago, Illinois 60611. Telephone : 312.787.2018, Fax : 312.649.9518.

Katherine McCoy

is CoChairman of Design at the Cranbrook Academy of Art in Bloomfield Hills, Michigan. As a partner in McCoy and McCoy she focuses on graphic design for cultural and educational clients, and she writes frequently on design. She recently coproduced a television documentary on Japanese design and completed the design of Cranbrook Design: The New Discourse, a book published by Rizzoli International. She is an elected member of the Alliance Graphique International, a Fellow in the Industrial Designers Society of America and currently serves as a vice president of the American Center for Design.

Faced with the prospect of chairing an annual competition, even one as distinguished as the 100 Show, I found myself once again questioning the current functionality and significance of the basic concept of an annual graphic design competition. Is it really possible to choose the best of a year's and a profession's graphic design output? How is design's relative success measured? How does one choose excellent design? In years past when our field was far less developed, it was fairly easy to determine the best of the field because even basic competency and graphic refinement was not all that common. Now graphic design/visual communications is a vast and highly evolved field. Virtually every entry received by a competition today demonstrates a high level of technical and stylistic sophistication. Professional competency is no longer a revelation.

What is an appropriate measure of the best today? Often "concept" and "innovation" are offered as criteria. Yet every juror has a personal interpretation of these words. How can one group of selections demonstrate a unified viewpoint of success chosen by a jury of strong individuals?

This brings up a second major question concerning juries. The process of consensus is problematic. Conventional communication design annual shows are chosen by group voting aimed at achieving an eventual consensus between jurors. Because juries have great difficulty agreeing on common standards, consensus

---

The American Center for Design is pleased to present the new 100 Show. The need to develop vehicles for critical review and analysis in design has become increasingly apparent in recent years. Their presence is an important characteristic of established professions. Thus we have seen, for example, a number of new professional design journals and an increasing number of professionally curated design exhibitions. Most design competitions, however, are juried; a group of **Robert Vogele** peers selects work by achieving a consensus. The limitations of this method are clear. The work that survives the process is typically safe and overproduced. Moreover, the passions of the jurors are canceled out, leading to a bland and predictable show. It is no wonder that one sees much of the same work in several of the leading competition annuals. The new 100 Show combines the best features of both curated exhibitions and juried competitions: a collection of important current work, plus the insight and critical analysis of Bruce Mau, Rick Vermeulen and Lorraine Wild. We are also pleased to introduce this year a look at the results of other major design competitions. Taken as a whole, this book is an important resource on trends and issues in design. We are excited about the new direction taken by the 100 Show. Special thanks to Katherine McCoy for her contributions to the 100 Show's continued success.

---

inescapably awards only the milder middle ground design on which all the judges can agree. Strong opinions cancel each other out. Often the fresher, riskier and generally less popular work falls through the cracks, resulting time after time in safe shows that fail to challenge, question or stimulate.

Perhaps the jury concept is irrelevant, given the present vast scale and sophistication of graphic design. Few fine art museums attempt such a concept. Rather, the critically-evolved field of fine art relies on curatorial shows to introduce notable new work and advance the field, relying on the insights and opinions of highly knowledgeable curators. Following this model, this year's 100 Show chose three distinguished jurors to act as curators and asked each to choose their own selections from the common pool of entries received. These jurors of distinctly different biases each curated one third of this year's 100 Show, based on three individual sets of criteria shaped by their personal design ethics and experiences. They were encouraged to be as biased as possible and to follow their personal convictions. Together these three visions of what mattered in communication design this year converge to form this distinctive show, shaped by curators rather than consensus, with no voting and no averaging. This process makes no claim to be an objective measure of 'the best' with which every designer in the country will agree. Rather, it is intentionally opinionated, uncovering new and significant work that the field of graphic design might not otherwise see.

In a sense this 100 Show is three shows in one, with the theoretical number of 100 divided by three. In practice, each juror had their own degree of inclusiveness and exclusiveness, so each has chosen a different number of pieces. The juror's selection reveals as much about the juror as about the graphic work chosen. To reveal each juror's personal interpretation and coherent vision, we have shown each as a section in this book.

With this process, the selection of jurors determined the tone of the show even more than in conventional competitions. We hoped to create an exhibition of work that would be provocative, something beyond what we see regularly, something that would predict emerging directions in design – even work that we might not immediately like because of its unfamiliarity or its difficulty. We sought jurors with highly informed, diverse viewpoints. Lorraine Wild's deep involvement with design history, design vernaculars and popular culture prepares her to consider the appropriate applications of historical forms and styles. Her interest in literary criticism and philosophy hone her critical viewpoint as well. Bruce Mau, a Canadian active in the Toronto art scene, has an active interest in contemporary fine art and artists. His design for books on fine art and contemporary culture demonstrate his acute sense of detail and typographic subtlety, a fresh view of minimalism in design form. Rick Vermeulen of Rotterdam, Netherlands, comes out of the rich Dutch cultural and political milieu. This social/cultural awareness shapes his strongly idiosyncratic work with energy and irreverence. This international jury reflects the increasingly international nature of visual communications. Although they all have corporate clients, the only quality they share in common is their design work for cultural clients and their willingness to let the cultures around them inform their work.

Our biggest concern was that in spite of their varied backgrounds and biases these three individuals would agree too much and choose the same pieces. In fact there were many overlaps in the first round of selections when each juror flagged work for a second look. As the selections were honed down, however, there were fewer overlaps, until the three jurors found only a few that they wished to show as true consensus pieces. These are featured together in this volume.

This submissions for this year's 100 Show revealed the state of the art to a large degree in this recessionary year. There were predictably fewer entries, yet most of the designers and design firms that regularly enter this competition did again this year. This may reflect fewer projects produced and lower budgets, and/or a hesitancy to spend large sums on entry and hanging fees.

At the same time there seemed to be a remarkably higher proportion of fresh work out of the mainstream, and a good percentage of this work was for hard-core commercial clients.The annual reports, for example, typically the most conservative section of any show, were far less formulaic and conservative. Business clients may be becoming more permissive and adventurous, or designers more courageous, daring to propose new formats and concepts. At the same time, there seemed not to be the usual reams of competent-but-typical work – pieces so slickly varnished that they slip out of the piles they are stacked in.

In the first round of selections, the jurors flagged at least twice the targeted number for the show, and all remarked that many projects eliminated in the later rounds seemed far better in quality than the typical winners of most shows. This would seem to be a very positive sign for graphic design. It seems that our field is again on the move. A number of new trends are beginning to come into focus. A new minimalism and restraint is beginning to show. Guilt and anxiety over the environmental costs of our work is stimulating new expressions. There is a new tangibility to graphic design, pieces that are good to feel and hold, as well as to look at. There were many small pieces that demanded a personal relationship with their viewers and that minimized consumption of resources. These frequently took the form of small books with traditional bindings and reproduction processes. This emphasis on craftsmanship over slick production techniques reflects a re-evaluation of hand processes as an antidote to the high degree of technology involved in today's graphic design.

Many pieces demonstrated an active involvement with the content on the part of the designer. There was evidence of the designer's writing in some of the copy. A responsibility for the content of the piece was demanded by each member of this jury. In several cases, pieces that initially attracted jurors were, on closer inspection, felt to be legitimizing flawed or fallacious client claims to altruism. There seemed to be agreement among these jurors that design is ultimately only as good as its message. A graphic piece cannot rise above a banal or troublesome message, no matter how beautiful or well-crafted.

Perhaps the most predominant change in evidence was the new restraint in graphic expression. Although some might be quick to attribute this to a return to the modernist minimalism of the Swiss School, the work seemed to defy such an easy explanation. The objective rationalism and neutral forms associated with "less is more" were not in evidence. The dictum "more into less", used by California designer (and teaching colleague of Lorraine Wild) Edward Fella, seems more appropriate. Much of the work selected for this year's 100 Show is subjective, ambiguous, subtle, interpretive and personal. Each speaks with a distinct and often eccentric voice, but these are restrained or quiet voices. Some pieces speak so softly, the whole room quiets down to hear – dramatically, even shockingly quiet.

This kind of work is not simple. All the lessons of the formal complexity of the postmodernism and New Wave of the 1970s and 1980s are embedded here. And there is a definite conceptual complexity. There is nuance, tone of voice, alternate and even conflicting voices, and self-critique in a lot of this work. Life is no longer simple, and neither are these graphic messages.

There is sensitivity in this restraint, a concern for the intimate relationship between the graphic piece and its audience. Jurors were observed fingering and stroking a number of the pieces, finding pleasure in their material qualities. Many of these pieces were deliberately small in scale to fit intimately in one's hand. Letterpress printing was used in a number of pieces; textural papers and additional strange materials were combined in very tactile expressions. These pieces require a firsthand primary experience and do not reproduce well in a publication such as this book. This is in marked contrast with more typical competition winners that exert their influence on the design community from the pages of annuals, often reduced to postage stamp sizes. This traditional type of work is extremely graphic, employing strongly defined images, sharp contrast and bright colors. Many of the pieces chosen this year call for direct contact between the communication artifact and its recipient. Perhaps there is a desire on the part of these designers to create communications that cannot be reproduced, replicated or digitized as a reaction or an antidote to the abstractions of the ongoing electronic information explosion and digital graphic design processes. This could be called a rematerialization of visual communications by designers living in a software world of computer interfaces. It is important to note that these material qualities involve our primal senses, bypassing the intellectual verbal decoding process of language.

At the same time, there is a great deal of language in much of this work, continuing a direction developed in recent years by a number of designers, including Thirst, M&Co., California Institute of the Arts and Cranbrook Academy of Art. Literary criticism, deconstruction theory and an interest in conversational texts have led to an exploration of verbal dynamics in visual communications: a typography of dialog and discourse, or aural typography. This approach to a complex typography requires a great deal of cerebral activity to "read" or decode the text's meaning. Imagery often seems to be downplayed in a lot of this kind of work, often reduced to symbols that must be 'read' as well. Perhaps it is partly as a compensating balance to all this verbiage that highly sensual preverbal elements of materiality have been introduced.

In addition to these conceptual characteristics, the entries shared a number of stylistic devices. Here are the awards for the clichés of the year based on rough counts during the judging process – and at least twenty percent could be added to each for the actual number. A quick count revealed 33 type-in-boxes devices and 26 type-in-ovals. As in recent years, brackets were popular (10) but not nearly as popular as the 38 checkerboards counted. Favorite compositional devices were color-fields-split-in-half at 32 and four-photos-butt-in-quadrants at 31. Certain symbols were de rigueur, including 26 spiked sun rays, 27 eyes, 36 hands and, the overwhelming favorite, 61 globes. (Evidence of the international nature of client messages and graphic design's global view? Or just a cool thing to do?) Often, more than two or three of these clichés were present on one piece. Graphic designers have long been notorious for their "sharing" of stylistic clichés, but seeing a year's graphic output gathered together drove that point home. Predictably, the jurors quickly became sensitized to the prevalence of certain clichés and avoided pieces bearing these devices unless the use of the element was conceptually defensible.

The body of entries in this year's 100 Show were cause for optimism. Notwithstanding a certain continuation of our field's predilection for slick production values and stylistic superficiality, there was a remarkable amount of fresh unpretentious work of intelligence and wit. A breath of fresh air seems to be blowing through our field at the moment. One can only hope it will contribute to a vigorous new period in the evolution of graphic design.

KM

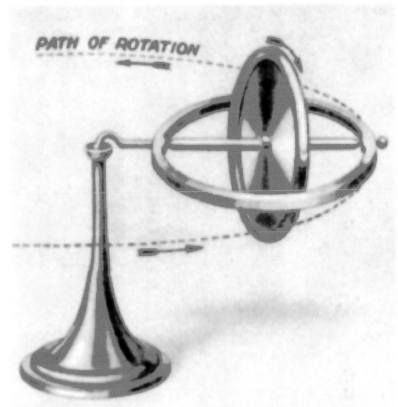

Juror

Essays

Lorraine Wild

teaches graphic design and design history at the California Institute of the Arts, where she is Director of Visual Communications. She lectures on design history, criticism and theory frequently and contributed a major essay to the book Graphic Design: A Visual Language History. She has been published widely, including ID Magazine, Print, Emigre, and the AIGA Journal. Her practice focuses on the design of architecture, fine art and design books for major museums and publishers, including the Museum of Contemporary Art in Los Angeles, Rizzoli International, and the MIT Press.

During the 1980s, the design profession underwent what might be called Competition Proliferation. Several new juried competitions were added to the old stand-bys like the New York Art Director's Club, the AIGA Book and Communication Graphics Shows, and the ACD 100 Show; perhaps this is a case where less actually is more. One of the by-products of this proliferation has been the development of a degree of cynicism on the part of many designers about the use/value of the numerous contests, old and new, and their many conventions: the high entry and hanging fees, the fuzzy criteria, the confusion of printing quality with design advancement, the weirdly provincial practice of allowing jurors to enter work, the postage-stamp sized reproductions in the annuals.

So it was with some trepidation that I agreed to serve on the jury of this year's ACD 100 Show, though I also felt that it was an honor to be asked, since this particular competition always seemed like one of the respectable ones (and tougher ones to place in, given the limit on the number of works chosen). The invitation was made more enticing by the agreement between the ACD and the show's chairperson,

---

BM **We saw quite a lot of good work,** it seems to me. In the first cut we selected maybe two hundred pieces. But then on the second look, when trying to find pieces that were consistent throughout, I read more closely and realized that something was missing from much of the work, that it didn't have the quality that I thought it had.

LW One aspect of a piece would be brought to the right level; but then, when you looked more closely, you would find the underpinning of the piece to be wobbly. This of course is the pitfall of most graphic design: the exterior is often very seductive, but it doesn't get you through a second look.

BM I also realized how rarefied a climate I work in, and how so much work in graphic design is not very demanding at all. There is so little work that really reflects the kind of culture that I am interested in, corporate or otherwise.

KM **Do you mean that most of the client messages** brought to designers are not really the kind of material you want to deal with?

BM Yes, because I don't think in terms of client messages.

RV **But you work for the client, don't you?**

BM Yes, but I don't think in those terms. If I take on a project, I take it on in a collaborative sense. I don't think in terms of target audiences or market segments or the kind of terminology that seems to be present in the work that we're seeing.

RV **But doesn't that sound more like art?** I mean, there is a difference.

BM When I went to visit this man in Italy to help him do some work, he asked me "Can you help? Can you tell me how to do this the way that you do it?" I said "I'll tell you how to do this if you tell me how to do art." His response was "There is no difference between what you do and what I do."

KM **This collaborative idea** might not necessarily be dysfunctional. Collaboration could serve the client's communication objectives perfectly well.

BM I think it has to. You must be delivering the product. In marketing terminology, you must be satisfying that client.

A Round Table DISCUSSION
WITH LORRAINE WILD, RICK VERMEULEN, AND BRUCE MAU
MODERATED BY KATHERINE MCCOY

Katherine McCoy, to eliminate the convention of jurying by consensus. I respect the two other jurors immensely, and looked forward to constructing a variation of the juried competition based on this experimental approach. It was going to be fun.

Not long before the jurying, I ran into Michael Beirut in New York, who told me that he had been kidding Kathy McCoy about inviting a jury that "promised to run the gamut from A to B!" Michael's thigh-slapper reminded me of the importance of trying to maintain some sort of objectivity (or at least to avoid acting out my own worst clichés) which of course was at odds with the whole curatorial direction that had been determined for this year's show. I began to suspect that our intention to "fix the format" would prove to be more complicated than we could possibly predict.

No amount of advanced planning quite prepares you for that first glimpse of a football-field sized room full of tables piled with print. I think we jurors quickly recognized that our experiment was about to be tested by two elements that had not been figured into the curatorial model: time (like all juries, we had only seconds to look at each piece, and to analyze whether it fit into our curatorial categories, or not), and selection (unlike curators, who slowly choose works for an exhibition from a theoretically infinite field, we had to choose from a field pre-determined by those who had sent in their work and paid their entry fees, whether they had actually read the published criteria or not).

All of this really did affect the jurying process. As I was inspecting each entry I realized that the work that I saw that was the most interesting (to me) was not necessarily in line with my announced criteria. For instance, this was not a big year for "history" (there was less quotation, appropriation, parody, or blatant rip-off). There was a lot of work that appeared to be informed by a knowledge of what has come before, but the issue of "history" just did not seem to jump out of the selections the way we thought it might, given that it was specifically noted in my juror's statement. But a juror's statement, of course, cannot really affect the character of the entries, since most of the entries are created long before the criteria are published. And, by and large, the work that was sent in was not radically different from previous years, reflecting the (vaguely disappointing) state-of-the-art, where the same sorts of projects elicit the same sorts of solutions, over and over again. Perhaps the published criteria did influence a small percentage of the pieces that entrants chose to submit, but I also think that we jurors adjusted our criteria during the process to work with the field of entries that faced us. The result of this friction between the jury's articulated standards and the actual work produced by the entrants is this very interesting hybrid of a show, something like a curated exhibition, but not really.

A note on the jurying process, at the risk of irritating my esteemed colleagues: it didn't quite work out as planned. Despite our different statements, we shared many opinions about the work. Though there were few pieces that all three of us agreed upon, there were lots and lots that two of us liked (in all combinations), but since we had agreed that we would maintain separate selections, we were forced into a sort of flea market, "I-saw-it-first" bartering which, in the end, created artificially larger distinctions between our three sets of choices. Designers whose pieces actually got two votes might be interested to know that; but that would have taken an additional, unforeseen clerical step in the jurying process that was already more complicated by the experiment. I explain this in hope that some future jury continues to tinker with the experiment (and to acknowledge how complicated it is to alter the competition formula).

The issue of time allotted for judging was really crucial to this show because all three of us jurors put such a high value on sense and appropriateness. (I know, from Michael Beirut's witticism, that because all three of us are known for book design and cultural institutional work, that it would be easy to accuse us of impractical artiness. But like myself, Mau and Vermeulen are pragmatists who suspiciously look first for the reason behind everything.) So we felt compelled to read into each entry as best we could. Many good-looking pieces were rejected; some because they were contentless, but more often because, upon closer inspection, content and form were at odds with each other.

LW **Some of what you're saying makes sense** about that ideal of collaboration between the designer and the client. It reminds me of advice that Paul Rand gave students at Yale: Never talk to anybody below the level of president. That's where we started in design: a designer would know the entrepreneur president of a company, and they would get together and work as peers (or at least this is the way it's always been described). That's how the seminal work in corporate communications was created. I think it was Tibor Kalman who pointed out that these days an assistant vice president of public relations is working with a representative of a design firm who is not necessarily the person actually at the board producing the work. It makes you wonder what went wrong when you see a good corporate annual report or corporate communications piece. What allowed something good to come out of the current system? Every successful firm reaches a point where they are faced with a choice between growth and control, whether they know it or not. They grow larger, yet seem to ignore the issue of whether they are still producing work as good as when they were smaller, the kind of work which initiated their growth.

KM **Then, occasionally, you do see a firm that just stops** and says, no, wait. And they downscale. I have seen several firms do that in recent years.

LW But you do sacrifice a certain economic success.

KM **Do you always? Is there a model** for this by which economic success isn't sacrificed?

RV I don't think there is.

BM When a firm grows, the quality must be dispersed, because you have to get people who can more or less copy your work to work in a similar manner. Then the quality of their work must be reduced somewhat because it's not a singular gesture, the sort that creates very powerful statements. This is what I'm dealing with in my own situation right now: how to do projects of a bigger scale.

RV If you work on your own, you do everything on the board from start to finish. If you have assistants, you have to think through a project before it actually starts.

KM **That might change your design process** because important thinking often happens while you are in the midst of the execution.

RV What we do a lot is a sort of combination: think beforehand, have the stuff done by someone else, and then finish it or jump in at some point.

KM Rick, you said earlier that you feel the designer should be held responsible for the content of the piece. We saw quite a few pieces that dealt with environmental issues and, in a few cases, social issues. What did you think about that work, and why did you reject some of it?

RV **It's very much a fashion.** A lot of firms get into environmental issues and recycled paper, and all that stuff to look good – to be nice, to do what

Graphic design is at a fascinating moment just now, where influences flow from the fringes into mainstream practice and back in the wake of postmodernism. But the old Achilles heel of graphic design still lingers: style-mongering that is inappropriate, or which just doesn't work, and its depressing corollary, good opportunities for design that go begging. (I don't feel that a banal message necessarily dooms a project to a banal form. I was as impressed by the designers who figured out how to make something visually compelling out of a beer-and-boxing promotion as I was by the designers who produced a visually compelling booklet on human rights activism. In both cases I suspect the designers took an aggressive role in the conceptual development of the works that they produced.) It seems clear that the only way graphic designers are going to continue to justify their existence is by applying the conceptual processes of design with as much intelligence, imagination and grace to all sorts of messages that we, as the audience, will continue to seek out (or endure). But the old issue of appropriateness (and now the newer one of environmental ethics) persists, no matter who the clients are.

In my teaching, I encounter students who think that competitions are so compromised that they should just be abolished. I don't agree with this because despite all of their limitations, they serve as vehicles for the development of an identity for graphic design. After going through this process, I think that the most troublesome aspect of competitions is the narrow range of projects entered, which is still probably influenced more by entry and hanging fees than it is by strategies for jurying. But I was more than happy to contribute to this effort to move the conventions of the competition, and while I don't think we achieved our ideal, I think that it is an improvement: at least this annual will produce a record of how and why each project was selected.

The reason that designers should continue to apply serious thinking to the competitions is that up to this point, by default, the competitions end up creating one of the few accessible historical records of the work that designers produce. As anyone who has tried to do research in design history knows, the first really serious difficulty encountered is the lack of archives. The incomprehensibly large realm of print actually serves as a barrier to understanding what graphic designers do. When one looks back at an old annual with a historian's eye (rather than as an entrant) one has to wonder first at what proportion of the total output of design is represented by its selections, and conversely, what it is that has been left out. Without any information from the jury, or responses from the entrants, those who seek to understand the choices made, and what they say about design at the time, simply will never know. What I saw in jurying this show is that a *salon des refuses* (a show of what was not selected) could have been just as interesting, organized around a different point of view, as the one that was selected.

clients and peers want. But one piece had fifteen color printing on recycled paper, for example.

LW **Another troubling example** was a piece on clean printing that used way too much paper. Another example is the printing of glossy Christmas booklets announcing that one is giving money to charity. (I must admit that I haven't done a piece printed with soy-based ink yet, but I'm going to have to soon because the Southern California air quality management district is going to require it.)

KM **I saw a direct** marketing brochure discussing all kinds of environmental issues and then concluding "make green your competitive edge."

LW **Well, we can be cynical, but** we do live in a capitalist society in which competitive edges are a very strong motivation. I hope that the consumer is getting smarter about what makes a product "green". The green consumer is ultimately going to reject this stream of junk mail.

RV Another thing: recycled paper looks recycled because it's fashionable. It doesn't have to look like recycled paper.

KM **So in terms of this green sensibility**, have you seen here a shift in attitudes towards materials, either in terms of quantity or in the nature of paper?

LW We are beginning to see it. It's definitely still in a nascent and confused stage.

KM **It is like all emerging technology,** quite rough around the edges at first. Did you see more uncoated, unbleached, or unrefined paper?

RV I saw a lot more here than in Europe.

LW **We saw a lot of paper company promotions** trying to sell recycled now that they finally see there is a demand. But it's one thing to get the promotion, and it's another thing to actually be able to procure the paper.

Supply is really a problem.

BM The consistency of the quality is also an issue. It's not resolved sufficiently.

KM **Recycled paper is an emerging technology too.** I understand that for a number of years a sizeable percentage of Japanese printing has been on recycled coated stock of quite an acceptable quality level. So my faith in technology assures me that the quality will come here too. Did you choose less slick work? How did you react to high production values with lots of glossiness as opposed to the more rough and less refined pieces?

RV **I selected less slick work** because I'm interested in that approach. Less slick can communicate as well as slick.

LW I tend to approach a extremely glossy piece with suspicion. I have to look for the thing that will prove to me that they really had to do it that way.

BM One thing that we noticed yesterday was the fact that so many people send in material for a competition like this that is highly produced because they think that's what design is. According to that view, simply produced work is not design.

KM **I've found during every jury** I've been on in recent years that about two-thirds of the way through the process all of the jurors almost simultaneously experience a backlash against high production values. When they come to a simple little one color or two color piece, everyone reaches for it. It's such a relief.

LW Yes, but you certainly don't see much evidence of that in annuals in the past few years. There are only a few shows you can name where the mold has been broken.

KM **People also do not** enter those simple pieces because they don't think that's what the jurors want to see.

A lot of frustration voiced about the limits of the juried competitions would be ameliorated by the appearance of more curated exhibitions that are not connected to competitions and which are more topical, like the exhibition produced by the Walker Art Center in 1989. That show raised a lot of controversy, mostly because design exhibitions are still such rare occurrences that they are unfairly expected to be encyclopedic. A similar critical burden is placed on competitions, which is why the ACD experimented with specificity this year. But on reflecting on our process, it is clear to me that the competition format has its limits. A proliferation of competitions, even reformed ones, cannot stand in for independently produced exhibitions and publications. Our field of graphic design has grown too big and interesting to be primarily described within the rules of these contests.

LW

Rick Vermeulen is a founding partner of Hard Werken [hard working in English], a multi-disciplinary design studio in Rotterdam, Netherlands. After experience with the renowned publisher Bert Bakker of Amsterdam, Rick co-founded Hard Werken Magazine with Gerard Hadders, out of which emerged the present studio of fifteen designers. Their work in corporate, cultural, governmental, editorial, packaging and interior design provokes both international acclaim and controversy for its outspoken design attitudes. Rick lectures on his work frequently in Europe and the United States.

Being a part of the jury for this year's 100 Show has been an exciting experience.

My interest in American graphic design culture dates back many years, even before I knew about design. I've always been very interested in American cultural and peripheral media output; things like typefaces, lettering, popular magazines, rock and roll, album covers, TV series, packaging, signage, etc. The periphery drew me inward to the "professional" design world.

In recent times, technological and electronic communication between Europe and the US has become easier, making it possible to produce a book, for instance, by fax, floppies and courier services in a week instead of a few months by post.

Exchange and mutual influence between Dutch and American schools and studios are starting to become a normal thing. During the last few years, I have visited the US often to teach/lecture, to see good friends in the design field or for other reasons. In the exchange of interests and ideas, I became more aware of American history, education, culture and communication. This exposure to both cultures made the judging more personally interesting.

I have a special interest in communicating simple ideas: Design is not art. Design should tell a well analyzed, understandable story. Design which costs a lot isn't necessarily more effective. Design should provide

LW The fact is there are a lot of one color pieces done by people who don't have any money and who look at the hanging fees with a degree of terror.

KM So there is some **Darwinian** natural selection going on.

LW I was surprised at the amount of self promotion work. I realize I am a bit naive; I think that people promote themselves through their work. On the other hand, I realize that I often hang on to things people send me that are expressions of themselves, because that has been a path for some time now to do things that they have not been able to do for client work. So self promotion seems to serve as an alternative channel.

RV **There is hardly any self promotion work in Europe**. You promote yourself through your work. Maybe that means all Europeans are lazy. I'm also used to seeing more art catalogs. Art catalogs in Holland exist because of their sponsorship by the government.

KM **Rick, how does American corporate** work compare with Dutch corporate work?

RV A couple of years ago it was completely different. But now the Dutch corporate work is looking more and more like American corporate work because of global corporations. It looks the same everywhere.

LW So there is a globalization of a corporate style?

RV Absolutely. It's a scheme.

BM I don't think there is really much difference between Canadian and American corporate work either. I would say there really is a globalizing tendency.

KM **Do you see any evidence** of regional styles?

LW Actually what I noticed was the spread of styles. There are now approximately four or five offices around the country doing a style that was once connected very much with Chicago, for example. There's a quick dissemination of formal influences, which obliterates the idea that

information. Design has to communicate. Design can communicate through entertainment. Design should be inventive. Design should be creative. Design has to be in and of the present. Design should not only be for designers. Design should be inspiring. Design should stimulate. Design could be prostitution. Design can be beautiful.

Something occurred to me during the judging. No matter who the client is, most corporate work has the same look: lots of color, lots of gloss, lots of varnish and, of course, the recycled paper section. Can a corporation belong to the club without printing its financial statements on recycled paper? I believe that by now, recycling should be routine, and I look forward to the day when you must print with vegetable-based inks to belong to the club.

I do believe in the connections between the arts, design, architecture, contemporary music, rock music, dance, theater, and movies. In recent years I have noticed a lot of "sampling" in the arts, particularly in the art form which uses the word as we now know it the most: house music.

Go into a studio with some recognizable albums and tapes, pick out some nice bits, reproduce them a couple of times, add some other instruments, or something eccentric of your own, mix it, and you have a new record. The only problem is that we haven't created anything new. Most of it is derivative. Take a successful formula, market it well and turn it into a global success. Just look at an act like Vanilla Ice. I hope the thaw will come soon.

Being inspired and influenced by others can be a great thing, a learning process that encourages you to go still further. We do not need another New Kids on the Block.

RV

American Center for Design FOURTEENTH ANNUAL 100 SHOW

Bruce Mau

of Toronto began his design work in the London office of Pentagram, after which he returned to Canada to co-found Public Good Design and Communication, specializing in social marketing. He currently practices independently on collaborative projects that present special challenges. His design of the ZONE series of books on cultural, social and philosophical issues has led him to explore broad concerns and specific ideas in depth. Other collaborations include the Getty Centre, The Carnegie Museum of Art, composer Gordon Monahan and architect Frank Gehry.

The tendencies I saw in the work for corporate clients reflected globalization. Most of this work was non-offensive, content free, ideologically unsound, and really cool looking. Much of the work made conspicuous use of environmentally-friendly materials, but it seemed to be because companies were afraid they would look silly if they didn't.

There's another interesting problem I think that's going to have to be dealt with in the coming few years, and that is how designers deal with the quality of images. The technology is now very good, and all the annual reports reflected that fact. They practically come off the end of an assembly line looking fabulous, full of great photography, great images, and beautiful printing. Museums and institutions that are concerned with the quality of images are going to have to decide what they are willing to live with. If you are really concerned about the quality of an image, you must also be willing to accept the fact that you will be working on virgin paper with highly toxic materials. I have worked with a coated recycled sheet that is really quite good, but as we all know, you never know what is going to happen on press.

there can be regional styles. It's been noticed for quite some time that the Print Regional Annual is not really regional.

KM **I'm trying to think if you could distinguish** Southern California from New England work. Sometimes the schools in a particular area and their graduates who stay on in the area will influence the look of the region's work to some extent.

LW **No, I think it's genres at work**: high corporate, medium corporate and low corporate. There is conservative culture, experimental culture, or institutional. There is the personalized, the neutral, and the coldly impersonal work. You can make a grid of those qualities in the genres of work. That to me would be a much more accurate way of describing or pinpointing a project rather then saying "That looks like it was made in Arkansas."

BM You just have to look at the graduates of Cal Arts and how they've dispersed. Mobility is now so great. There are also people who are working in many places simultaneously.

RV But do you think that's good? Or an example of globalization?

BM **In my case, it tires me out.**

RV I think it's interesting to see that some work comes from a certain place. If I go to France I can buy a nice bottle of French wine, for instance, but I can also get it anywhere. I can get everything everywhere. It's the same sort of thing that applies to design as well. Communication is so fast, it becomes one big mess. That's what I don't like about global design. The same things are happening everywhere and you don't get inspiration anymore from Italy, from California or from Germany. There's a sort of leveling out.

BM **But I still think you have local design communities** that work within themselves. I think there's still a recognizable Dutch style, for example. There is kind of an internal working mechanism that spins the thing around and generates a local vernacular. It gets dispersed quite easily, in fact, through processes like this competition.

If you have ever been at the end of a press, you know why this is an issue. But where does this issue fit in the overall mix of how we deal with production and reproduction in our culture? Designers still have no understanding, for example, of how to deal with the sludge that is extracted during the recycling process. There are real costs to making a recycled thing, and there is very little if any willingness to deal with the issues of overproduction and overconsumption.

I still believe that designers should promote things they believe in; that they should use their work to further ideas, causes, technologies, and businesses that they think are doing good things; and that they should be closely connected to the content of their work.

Pieces with really good content were at a premium. I think the work reflects a murky time. In order to make a clear image of a statement, you need a clear statement to begin with.

BM

LW I was thinking about how both Interview and Beach Culture ended up being selected by all of us. In fact, they're almost the same. You could make an argument, however, that Interview is a tight, New York, media-based, highly produced version of an attempt to make minimalist typography speak without indulging in histrionics; and that Beach Culture is taking those same formal elements and falling off the continent with it. The truth is, when you look at Beach Culture you think of attenuated surfer slang.

BM The one is avoiding histrionics, and the other is trying to make the histrionics minimal.

KM Did you find that you chose things that were similar or different from your own work?

BM Certainly I chose some things that were similar, because I liked them. But I chose some things that I would never do in my whole lifetime.

LW I can't even imagine having the opportunity to do a Budweiser piece for a boxing match. The lack of good content was really noticeable because of current trends in typography where messages are emphasized. When the messages are nothing you get this well-articulated disappointment.

RV Some pieces really looked nice, with hundreds of layers of typography, but we didn't know what they meant or what they were about. I saw a lot of confusing reports and brochures with a lot of layering. It's more image building. But you have to really sit down and look in order to figure it out. Global design sampling. The blurry image.

KM Are you issuing a call for clarity?

RV Definitely, a call for clarity.

KM Is that a sort of return to Bauhaus principles?

RV I think that if you are going to communicate through print work it should be legible, with the kind of clarity you should be looking for and waiting for.

LW From what I can tell as a teacher, we are at the top of the curve, or maybe even starting to go down, as far as tolerance for that level of complexity is concerned. Clarity is seen not as being simple, one message, the big symbol; but rather as trying to get more into fewer elements. Not making the message dumb, but rather just doing it with a little less. In a way, it becomes part of the issue we all are facing right now regarding consumption and overuse in our culture.

KM The modernist ideal was not only clarity but also objectivity. It seems like designers might be working towards clarity but still wanting to retain ambiguity and breadth of interpretation.

LW I don't think we can go back again. It gets to this issue of the designer's role, the designer's voice, whether you have a voice in the work, whether your intentions become part of the work. To suddenly go back to the old ethic and say I'm not really there, I'm just going to point the way to a perfect objectivity, is just not going to happen. There is nothing else in our culture that works that way.

KM Or when it does seem to be clear, it in fact turns out to be oversimplified and therefore has no integrity. We live in a complex world.

Selections

JURORS' **Consensus**

SELECTIONS

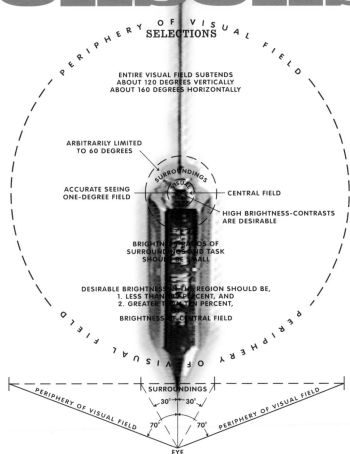

PERIPHERY OF VISUAL FIELD

**ENTIRE VISUAL FIELD SUBTENDS
ABOUT 120 DEGREES VERTICALLY
ABOUT 160 DEGREES HORIZONTALLY**

**ARBITRARILY LIMITED
TO 60 DEGREES**

SURROUNDINGS

VISUAL

**ACCURATE SEEING
ONE-DEGREE FIELD**

CENTRAL FIELD

**HIGH BRIGHTNESS-CONTRASTS
ARE DESIRABLE**

**BRIGHTNESS RATIOS OF
SURROUNDINGS AND TASK
SHOULD BE SMALL**

**DESIRABLE BRIGHTNESS IN THE REGION SHOULD BE,
1. LESS THAN 60 PERCENT, AND
2. GREATER THAN TEN PERCENT,**

BRIGHTNESS OF CENTRAL FIELD

PERIPHERY OF VISUAL FIELD

PERIPHERY OF VISUAL FIELD

SURROUNDINGS

30° 30°

70° 70°

PERIPHERY OF VISUAL FIELD

PERIPHERY OF VISUAL FIELD

EYE

Darin Pappas BEACH CULTURE MAGAZINE

ENTRANT'S COMMENTS

An article about an artist who takes old, discarded surfboards and turns them into beautiful pieces of art.

David Carson — DESIGNER

Carson Design — DESIGN FIRM

Beach Culture — CLIENT

Carson — TYPOGRAPHER

Maxwell — PRINTER

American — SEPARATOR

Inform and educate — OBJECTIVES

Consumer — AUDIENCE

David Lynch, Unearthed BEACH CULTURE MAGAZINE

ENTRANT'S COMMENTS

This was the first professional interview ever done with David Lynch. In looking at Lynch's work, there seemed to be a lot of subtleness and breaking of the rules. Hence, the page number [34] is larger than the title itself, and the second column of type is centered directly over the gutter, which is saddlestitched with staples. To have gone loud, crazy or bizarre would have been too obvious a call.

Neil Feineman — WRITER

Jan Weinberg — PHOTOGRAPHER

Hanging at Carmine St. BEACH CULTURE MAGAZINE

ENTRANT'S COMMENTS

The title seemed like a good opportunity to hang some type.

Pat Blashill — WRITER

Pat Blashill — PHOTOGRAPHER

Surfing Blind BEACH CULTURE MAGAZINE

ENTRANT'S COMMENTS

This was an opening spread for an article on teaching blind people how to surf. In the bottom right hand corner the word "more" appears, but the continuation of the story was placed randomly in the back of the magazine, making it difficult for the reader to find.

Night Before Last   BEACH CULTURE MAGAZINE

PHOTOGRAPHER

Steve Sherman

ENTRANT'S COMMENTS

This was an article by a writer who contrasted two groups of similarly aged people from different cultures. One night the writer attended a Rap concert in Los Angeles; the next night the Russian Ballet performed in San Diego. The image on the left is a symbol very common to Rap in general, and the Rap group Public Enemy in particular. On the right is a photo taken during the Russian Ballet. Contrast was the main design theme here. The article began on the next page.

Surf Trip   BEACH CULTURE MAGAZINE

ENTRANT'S COMMENTS

Opening spread of an article about a writer who ventures into Mexico, supposedly on a "surf trip", who experiences many non-surf-related events on his journey.

The Last Hold Out   BEACH CULTURE MAGAZINE

ENTRANT'S COMMENTS

PHOTOGRAPHER

Steve Sherman

The old and the new. The article is about the last family to give in to developers and move off land that had been in the family for hundreds of years. The "e" is from Herbert Bayer, and is surrounded by newer, "designer" fonts: the "th" from Japan, "last holdout" from Berkeley. The "e" became much like the home pictured in the layout that was being surrounded by condos and "attached single family" dwellings.

BM

It looks so loose but in fact the timing of the words is very well controlled. The folding of text into itself is really smartly resolved. Very sharp.

LW

It has this incredible physical reference to the turning and twisting of water and surfing. The reading direction of the page, how you are supposed to look at this, is actually always ambiguous.

RV

What I like about Beach Culture is that it has a completely amateur feel to it. You know it's not amateur if you look through it. But it looks like someone discovered a computer and went crazy.

Interview Magazine

ENTRANT'S COMMENTS

Interview is about people revealing themselves through conversation. The typography, whether body copy, excerpted, quoted, or headlines, is meant to reveal the tone, color and content of the subject's voice. Type is mute. We mean to give it voice.

DESIGNERS
Tibor Kalman, Kristin Johnson
DESIGN FIRM
M&Co.
CLIENT
Interview
TYPOGRAPHER
Interview
OBJECTIVES
Inform and educate, document
AUDIENCE
Consumer

BM

It pulses as you read. It throbs. That's what's so rigorous about it: it actually functions better as a text than as an image. They've managed to create an identity for the publication, something very difficult to do. It puts a smart spin on pop culture, maybe smarter than the magazine itself. It definitely shows people in their best light.

LW

The Athol Fugard spread is one of the more interesting typographic compositions in the show. It's "talking type" that we are all used to, but it has a discipline of the means which makes you read it and see it very clearly. The art direction is done with an incredible eye. The truth is, in content it's airplane reading. But if I'm going to have my pop cultural fix, I'd rather have it this way than with a piece of tabloid junk.

RV

I responded to the whole magazine, the approach, rather than any specific spreads. The spreads are more like posters. Put one on your wall for a couple days and look at it. Replace it with another spread. You don't need a large format to make this kind of statement.

My Hard Bargain Dust Jacket

ENTRANT'S COMMENTS

In the first story of this collection, a group of adolescent boys in a Mormon school is asked by their teacher/basketball coach to keep track of how many times they masturbate by marking an ultraviolet star each time on a large piece of black paper. At the end of the season, the coach assembles the team, posts all the papers, and in the darkened locker room, turns on a big black light. The story is called "Planetarium". All the photography was done on the photostat camera. The spin is the best part.

DESIGNER

Chip Kidd

ART DIRECTOR

Carol Devine Carson

WRITER

Walter Kirn

PHOTOGRAPHER

Chip Kidd

CLIENT

Alfred A. Knopf, Inc.

TYPOGRAPHER

Kidd, Photolettering

PRINTER

Coral Graphic

SEPARATOR

Coral Graphic

PAPER

White Wash 3

OBJECTIVES

Generate inquiry, document

AUDIENCE

Consumer

BM

This has a very nice filmic quality that unfolds in time the way that you experience the book. The interactions of the images as a kind of montage is really well resolved here. Beautifully done.

LW

The shifts off the format of the book, particularly on the spine, are great.

RV

The image actually wrapping around onto the middle of the flap is wonderful. I also like the yellow dot over the bar code. There are a number of details that are very well executed.

Past Lives ARTIST'S BOOK

ENTRANT'S COMMENTS

Past Lives was a true collaboration; all brought a compatible interest and enthusiasm to the project. A mutual respect allowed us to do what we as individuals do best, and collectively more than any one person could have done. The book's subject matter, American pop vernacular of childhood and the recent past, was particularly interesting from a graphic design standpoint. The question was how to use nostalgic and pop-vernacular imagery without falling into those stylistic clichés. What I tried to do was keep the overt stylizing to a minimum and be as direct and honest to the feel of the original material as possible. I studied a lot of children's books and tried to convey a sense of them without sentimentalizing or condescending. Making no attempt to stylistically re-contextualize, I also treated the artist's photographs and collages in a straightforward manner, allowing the reader to draw their own conclusions. In the end, I think the design is nostalgically sentimental and condescendingly sarcastic, as well as funny/sad, pretty/ugly, and smart/dumb, and this plurality makes it utterly contemporary.

DESIGNER

Mr. Keedy

WRITERS

Amy Gerstler, Alexis Smith

CLIENT

Santa Monica Museum of Art

TYPOGRAPHER

Mr. Keedy

PRINTER

Donahue Printing Co.

OBJECTIVE

Artist book to accompany exhibition

AUDIENCE

Consumer

BM

This level of collaboration yields very unusual results. That's the thing that raises this above the rest of the material. From a distance, as a designer, you probably wouldn't have the courage to do these things to someone else's work. But when you get in close and you have that collaborative process, an opening is created and you are able to move into that space.

LW

It's a document of an exhibit, but it's not like the exhibit; it's a different piece, it's become a work of its own. It's really fascinating when considered as a model for how to do an exhibition catalog, and its visual quality is wonderful.

RV

Almost every page is independently designed, but it's all linked together. It's one piece.

Social Responsibility and the Design Professions SEMINAR ANNOUNCEMENT

The goal of the seminar was to replace the faded, superficial architectural/urban planning discourse of the 1980s with a renewed concern for social change. In designing the event's announcement, I created a composition of Herbert Bayer influenced arrows, rich with scientific and diagrammatic associations, to abstractly represent evolution, energy, and change. Barry Deck's lettering template inspired font Template Gothic reinforces the architect's role in the discourse as do such details as the alignment of the title's three I's through the center fold.

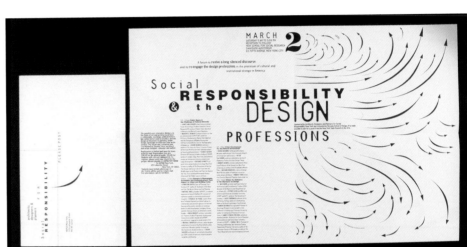

DESIGNER

Barbara Glauber

WRITER

Susana Torre

DESIGN FIRM

Heavy Meta for Two Twelve Associates

CLIENT

Architects, Designers and Planners for Social Responsibility

PRINTER

Royal Offset

OBJECTIVES

Generate inquiry, inform and educate, introduce

AUDIENCES

Architecture, design professionals

American Center for Design FOURTEENTH ANNUAL 100 SHOW

BM

The left half is a very seductive image. Every graphic designer in America will love this because it's just a beautiful thing, and that to me carries the day.

LW

A lot of my positive reaction to this piece has to do with what it's not. It's not overwrought. It has a simple message with a strong typographic presence that is meant to attract the attention of the audience it's directed to without indulging in gloss and overproduction. The form is appropriate to the message and the audience.

RV

It's simple and beautifully executed. The typography is very nicely done, but it's not too special.

Unherd of Productions Logo

Actually, this didn't begin as a logo assignment. The client hired me to design a letterhead and had envisioned a type treatment of some kind. The pun in the company's name was a hook, but I wasn't coming up with anything very satisfying in type. The image of a TV was an obvious choice to represent their business (video production) so I experimented with it as well as type. A cartoon-like sketch of a TV I had made on my tracing pad triggered the recognition of a visual pun to match the verbal.

DESIGNER
Ron Kellum

ILLUSTRATOR
Ron Kellum

DESIGN FIRM
Ron Kellum Design

CLIENT
Unherd of Productions

OBJECTIVES
Generate inquiry, introduce

AUDIENCE
Corporate

LW
I think we're tired of the usual, clichéd abstract logos. This has an animated quality to it and yet is still well within the genre of the contained mark. The wit and energy of the drawing somehow got retained as it got simplified.

BM
I couldn't agree more.

RV
It's playful and humorous, and yet is everything a logo should be at the same time.

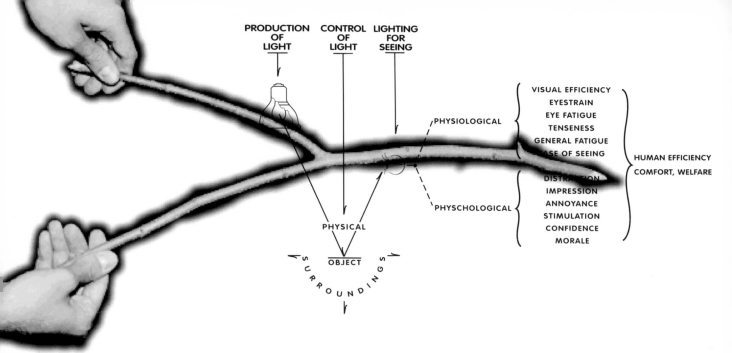

PRODUCTION OF LIGHT

CONTROL OF LIGHT

LIGHTING FOR SEEING

PHYSIOLOGICAL

VISUAL EFFICIENCY
EYESTRAIN
EYE FATIGUE
TENSENESS
GENERAL FATIGUE
EASE OF SEEING

HUMAN EFFICIENCY
COMFORT, WELFARE

PHYSICAL

PHYSCHOLOGICAL

DISTRACTION
IMPRESSION
ANNOYANCE
STIMULATION
CONFIDENCE
MORALE

OBJECT

SURROUNDINGS

LORRIANE **Wild** SELECTIONS

The ABCs of ▲■●:
The Bauhaus and Design Theory

ENTRANT'S COMMENTS

This project brings together our work as writers, editors, and designers. Each essay in the book uses the grid and typographic elements in a distinct way to reflect its specific content. The subject of the book is modernism, and we have tried to use both design and writing as media for exploring the modernist syntax.

DESIGNERS

Ellen Lupton, J. Abbott Miller, Mike Mills

ART DIRECTOR

Ellen Lupton

EDITORS

Ellen Lupton, J. Abbott Miller

PHOTOGRAPHER

Joanne Savio

DESIGN FIRM

Herb Lubalin Study Center

CLIENT

Herb Lubalin Study Center

TYPOGRAPHERS

Ellen Lupton, J. Abbott Miller

PRINTER

Red Ink Productions

PAPER

Warren Lustrolux Dull

OBJECTIVES

Inform and educate, document

AUDIENCE

Consumer

LW

This book is interesting for its interpretation of basic modernist typography. It also offers some very interesting documentation, particularly of the precursors to various Bauhaus projects, such as the kindergarten projects of the turn of the century. It's a spectacular piece of research and a real resource. The Herb Lubalin Study Center is to be lauded.

The Actual Adventures of
Michael Missing: Dust Jacket

This is a book of short stories loosely connected by the same character (narrator) throughout. Michael is many things: pirate, child, baseball player, gunsmith, worm collector, rapist, pig. I designed it immediately, sans drawings. I wanted someone who drew like Charles Burns to work on it. I couldn't find anyone. Weeks passed. Carol Carson, art director, advised that I call Charles Burns and ask him to do it; an irrefutable suggestion. I had illustrations in 3 days. This is one of the few jackets for which I was allowed to design the flaps and back ad. It is complete.

DESIGNER

Chip Kidd

ART DIRECTOR

Carol Devine Carson

WRITER

Michael Hickins

ILLUSTRATOR

Charles Burns

CLIENT

Alfred A. Knopf, Inc.

TYPOGRAPHER

Kidd, Photolettering

PRINTER

Coral Graphic

PAPER

Opulant Chrome White

OBJECTIVES

Generate inquiry, document

AUDIENCE

Consumer

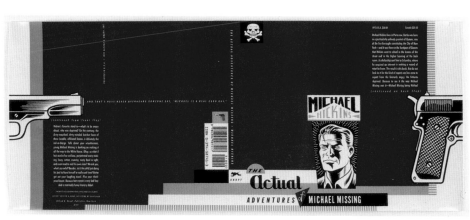

LW

This book cover uses a kind of vernacular, the line cut, bad 1930s or 1940s illustration, and "ironic" typography, that we see used very frequently by Charles Anderson or the Duffy Group; but this designer pulls it apart, deconstructs it, so it becomes something much more contemporary. This is a wonderful example of playing with a historical style and liberating it from its own past, doing something so odd to it that is not just a simple mimicry of the style. You can't call this version of that vernacular mere appropriation; this manipulation becomes something quite original and interesting.

April in April Poster

ENTRANT'S COMMENTS

This is an announcement and documentation for a presentation by April Greiman. Design elements included word plays and images of water and flowers, Los Angeles, Women in Design, the Pacific coast, and membership attendance.

DESIGNER
James A. Houff

PHOTOGRAPHER
Paul Price

DESIGN FIRM
James A. Houff Design

CLIENT
AIGA/Detroit

PRINTER
Typocraft

SEPARATOR
Precision Color

PAPER
Warren Lustro Dull

OBJECTIVES
Generate inquiry, inform and educate, document

AUDIENCES
Consumer, membership

LW

This is another example of a designer taking a style from very contemporary history, but in his way pushing it one step further. It's almost a "higher res" version of what April might do in a different media. What is also so cool about this poster is that it plays with the obvious pun, "April in April", the "April showers bring May flowers" cliché (which in Detroit really connects to spring), and the visual interpretation of April Greiman's style. The more you look at this poster, the better it gets in terms of its sophisticated conjunction of the obvious pun and the style.

The formal structure of the book refers to Art Center's distinctive architecture. The catalog's length and open spatial aspect refers literally to the building and metaphorically to the openness of the educational process. The captions throughout echo the process of intellectual inquiry that parallels the aesthetic vision. The reader's sensory experience is heightened through the book's elasticity. It yields and bends to the touch; its uncoated stock absorbs imagery rather than defining it sharply. The active, emotional, process-oriented editorial photography depicts everyday student life in an uncontrolled style, in direct contrast to the controlled, formal, product-oriented images of completed student work. The choice of Gill Sans type gives a warm, organic feeling, a conscious shift in direction from the Helvetica used in Art Center recruitment catalogs of the past.

DESIGNER

Rebeca Mendez

ART DIRECTORS

Rebeca Mendez, Stuart J. Frolick

WRITERS

Stuart J. Frolick, Karen Jacobson

PHOTOGRAPHERS

Steven A. Heller, Eika Aoshima

DESIGN FIRM

Art Center College of Design,
Design Office

CLIENT

Art Center College of Design

TYPOGRAPHER

Dee Typographers

PRINTER

Colorgraphics

SEPARATOR

Colorgraphics

PAPER

Columbia, Dulcet

OBJECTIVES

Inform and educate

AUDIENCE

Prospective students

LW

Art college catalogs are incredibly difficult to design. The thing that distinguishes this one is the very careful and elegant typographic approach. The contrast of impressionistic images along with the very crystalline and carefully chosen images of student work make this catalog quite interesting. It also allows you to look through it strictly as a picture book without getting into the details, addressing the confusion that these catalogs typically have between functioning as promotional items and functioning as yearbooks. The hierarchical typography allows it to function both ways without clouding the view of the reader who is not familiar with the school.

Beowulf: A Likeness

ENTRANT'S COMMENTS

The "Beowulf: A Likeness" project is an entrepreneurial experiment that integrates many kinds of design: the literary design of Beowulf, the design of a concept about Beowulf, and finally, how that concept is given visual form and brought to market. I do not conceive of the book's imagery as illustrating the text, but as a separate system of meditations that interprets the volume's cohering vision. Reproductions of pages from the 10th century Anglo-Saxon manuscript are part of a visual system that runs throughout the volume. They surface as light images behind Raymond Oliver's retelling of Beowulf to remind the reader that "Beowulf: A Likeness" is a retelling of a tale that, in turn, was retold by the orginal Anglo-Saxon author. The manuscript pages periodically submerge under images of geography and artifacts during certain narrative segments, and then surface again to reassert the presence of the original Anglo-Saxon text. At times the manuscript pages literally visually transform and enter into a sort of direct collaboration with the history and action they symbolize.

DESIGNER
Randy Swearer

WRITERS
Randy Swearer, Raymond Oliver, Marijane Osborn, Fred Robinson

ILLUSTRATORS
Randy Swearer, Kate Breakey

PHOTOGRAPHERS
Randy Swearer, Kate Breakey

DESIGN FIRM
Randy Swearer Design

PUBLISHER
Yale University Press

TYPOGRAPHER
Highwood Type Services

PRINTER
Rembrandt Printing

PAPER
Warren Lustro Dull

OBJECTIVES
Inform and educate

AUDIENCE
Consumer

LW

The designer illuminated an existing text by interpreting it visually. It really does work, through a very seductive and yet quite historically accurate set of images which place the ancient story in its context. It is much more than another illustrated version of the poem. He provides a whole set of visual footnotes which expand the interpretation of the epic. This is a model project in which a designer initiated a publication because of his own interest in the subject and ability to produce it.

Brainstorm

Brainstorm introduces a new service which produces a custom designed product, or a customized stock item, in large quantities for multiple commercial spaces. The book serves to stimulate creative thinking in the minds of architects, interior designers and other participants in the creative transformation of interior environments. Brainstorm introduces a design process that involves both designers and technicians. The presentation proposes the synthesis of technical expertise in product development with the creative surge of the design process. The book begins by breaking down preconceptions of the creative process. It then forces the reader to rethink previous conceptions of environment and space. The reader is asked to imagine a process that synthesizes creative and technical thinking into a single product development process. The book then finally outlines the process. This is presented through imagery, prose, and poetry printed on transluscent paper, teasing and enticing the reader.

DESIGNER
Mark Oldach

WRITER
Marlene Marks

PRODUCTION
Rachel Schreiber

ILLUSTRATOR
David Csicsko

PHOTOGRAPHER
Alan Shortall

DESIGN FIRM
Mark Oldach Design

CLIENT
USG Interiors

PRINTER
First Impression

PAPERS
Gilbert Gilclear, Gilbert Neutech

OBJECTIVES
Generate inquiry, support of sales

AUDIENCES
Architects, interior designers

LW

This commercial announcement is reminiscent of a very well done graphic design school project. The word "brainstorm" is extrapolated through a very poetic essay with words and pictures on the idea of "brain", on "storm", on "brainstorm", on every possible implication of those words. It ends up also being about thinking and communication as a process. It's a spectacular, heavy, beautifully printed piece, almost over-produced. There's nothing modest or inexpensive about it. On the other hand, the poetry of the piece makes up for the excess of the production.

The Citadel

Built on the site of what was once the largest tire factory on the west coast, The Citadel, a 35-acre mixed-use center, is a collision of low-tech industrial elements and Hollywood fantasy. The Citadel's graphics and identity program extends this collision. Built in 1929, the 1,700 foot "Assyrian" wall and ziggurat-shaped administration building are a well-known landmark to hundreds of thousands of passing motorists. Friezes on the wall inspired the logo (an Assyrian winged lion with a man's head known as a lammasu) as well as the stylized, sculptural archers made of unpainted steel that occupy one of the project's retail plazas. Invoking a more directly industrial mythology, an off-the-shelf utility tower provides the framework for a 140-foot sign that identifies the retail center behind the wall to passing motorists. Spinning tires atop the retail center's main directory evoke the site's orginal purpose.

DESIGNER

Deborah Sussman

ART DIRECTOR

Fernando Vazquez

WRITERS

Scott Cuyler, Ena Dubnoff, Kyoko Tsuge, Holly Hampton

PHOTOGRAPHERS

Derek Rath, Jeremy Samuelson, Annette Del Zoppo Photography

DESIGN FIRM

Sussman/Prejza & Co., Inc.

CLIENT

Trammell Crow Company

OBJECTIVES

Identify and direct visitors, enhance experience

AUDIENCES

Corporate, consumer

LW

This is a very imaginative use of highly ornamental signage in a situation where it doesn't usually appear; in this case, an industrial and retail outlet situated next to a historic building. Because the building is overwhelming in its "neo-Babylonian" style, there are really only two ways to approach it: either to do something quiet and neutral which stands away from its style or to play with the same goofy stylistic fantasy style which was obviously behind the original design of the building. There appear to be two kinds of signs: one for the real estate, which has a kind of art deco interpretation, and a more eclectic group for the actual outlet collection itself. There are all kinds of strange motifs: Assyrian archers for the sign posts, a directory with the floating tires on top. It's a funny addition of stylistic vernaculars to a spot that already had a very odd mix. The styles match the architecture without being slavish. What's funny is how the designers had nerve to actually add to the stylistic mish-mash of the original: they recognized that consistency here called for no consistency at all.

ENTRANT'S COMMENTS

The cable television industry is saddled with a host of preconceived notions. As the third largest US cable television operator, Comcast wanted to set itself apart and to do so we used the very arguments often leveled against the cable industry. The humorous and ironic effects were acheived through first seeing the paradox in its negative form and then opening the gatefold to reveal the opposite, and then coupling them with surprising imagery from a variety of cable television programs (sports, cartoons, music videos, movies, news, etc.).

DESIGNER

Riki Sethiadi

ART DIRECTORS

Danny Abelson, Aubrey Balkind,
Kent Hunter

WRITER

Danny Abelson

EXECUTIVE PHOTOGRAPHY

Bill Duke

DESIGN FIRM

Frankfurt Gips Balkind

CLIENT

Comcast Corporation

TYPOGRAPHER

Frankfurt Gips Balkind

PRINTER

Lebanon Valley Offset

PAPER

Potlach Vintage Velvet

OBJECTIVES

Generate inquiry, inform and
educate, introduce, support of sales

AUDIENCES

Corporate, internal, consumer,
shareholder

American Center for Design FOURTEENTH ANNUAL 100 SHOW

LW

The engaging thing about this piece is the double-reading trick used throughout, where there's a half-page added to spreads that transforms photographs into a humorous counterpoint to the text. It's very thoughtful design, more lively than the typical annual report.

Communication in Architecture
BROCHURE

ENTRANT'S COMMENTS

This served as a marketing piece for the architectural firm Ellerbe Becket, headquartered in Minneapolis, with several offices around the country. Based on interviews with its prominent architects, our collaboration seamed together good and bad architecture, good and bad photography, and good and bad typography into some kind of pop elegance aimed at potential corporate clients.

DESIGNERS
P. Scott Makela,
Laurie Haycock Makela

EDITOR
Cathy Bogerly

DESIGN FIRM
Commbine, Cranbrook

CLIENT
Ellerbe Becket, Inc.

TYPOGRAPHER
Key Tech

PRINTER
Typocraft

OBJECTIVE
Generate inquiry

AUDIENCE
Consumer

LW

This in-house publication for an architecture firm breaks away from the typical nervously straightforward display of work that most architecture firms produce. Visually, it produces a dialog with the partners of this firm on precisely what it is they are trying to accomplish in their work. The typography and layout communicate the idea of the working process. There is humor in the use of the photographs of the architect's mouths next to the headline "Communication in Architecture", but it isn't dumb humor; it really is about the kind of directness and candor that goes on in a meeting. The typography is almost aggressively clear, and would just have to hook a potential client into reading the text. This intimate and talkative style is unusual in architectural materials and is a real contribution on the part of the designers.

Cuba-USA INVITATION

ENTRANT'S COMMENTS

This broadside invites donors to the Museum of Contemporary Art to an opening of a group exhibition of Cuban émigré artists living in the United States. An invitation for a group exhibit should broadly represent the show, rather than featuring the work of only one or a few of the artists represented. Additionally, we wanted to depart from the usual panel-card-type invitation for this exclusive opening. By mimicking silkscreened broadsides and by printing on inexpensive stock using a local "fast printer", this design refers to a lively tradition of street graphics evident in Latin American communities in the United States. If not actually addressed to a multicultural audience, the invitation signals an increasing effort on the part of the museum to address different contents from diverse cultures, rather than limiting itself to the Euro-American modernism that has dominated so much of 20th century art.

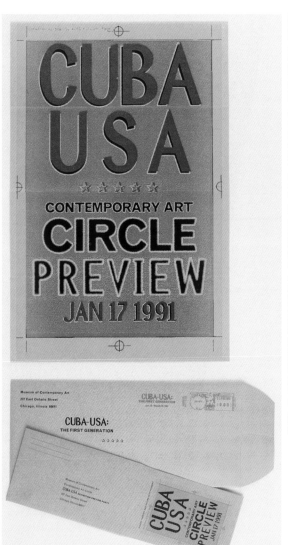

DESIGNER

John Calvelli

WRITER

David Luckes

CLIENT

Museum of Contempory Art

TYPOGRAPHER

ProTypography

PRINTER

Sir Speedy

PAPER

Wausau

OBJECTIVES

Generate inquiry, invite members to an art opening

AUDIENCE

Museum Circle members

LW

The casualness and contemporaneity of this piece make it very alluring. It doesn't even begin to hint at what the art in the exhibit looks like. The color choices are fascinating; there's no attempt to deal with classic patriotic colors, but one might say that the pink, aqua and purple are patriotic colors that have undergone a transformation. (I'm reminded of the jokes about "pinkos".) I also find the cast shadow behind the "Cuba-USA" typography to be an interesting element from a kind of signage vernacular, but which in this case might reflect the shadowy influence of two countries on each other. At first glance this looks like a telephone pole poster, yet the more you look at it, the more you realize that the sophisticated typography carries all kinds of wonderful, fuzzy implications for what you might find in the exhibit. All of the pieces teeter on the edge of non-design, an interesting condition where the designer loads many different gestures which tread the line between being obvious and being something that could be strictly in the reader's interpretation.

A Thousand Points of Departure
POSTER

This poster was designed to announce a lecture by Ralph Caplan on the work of Charles and Ray Eames to members of AIGA/San Francisco. I wanted to create a dynamic image that would convey the eclectic nature and vitality of the Eames' work to get people excited about coming to this event. Caplan's lecture was to focus on the Eames' problem-solving approach rather than be a visual presentation of their work. Consequently, the poster evolved into a metaphor for the design thought process, utilizing the Eames' work (in graphics, film, furniture, interiors and exhibitions) as "points of departure" emanating from the designer's mind. The angled trim of the poster was intended as a point of departure from the traditional rectangle.

DESIGNER
Earl Gee

WRITER
Ralph Caplan

ILLUSTRATOR
Earl Gee

DESIGN FIRM
Earl Gee Design

CLIENT
AIGA/San Francisco

SPONSOR
Herman Miller, Inc.

TYPOGRAPHER
Omnicomp

PRINTER
AR Lithographers

SEPARATOR
NovaColor

PAPER
Simpson Coronado SST

OBJECTIVES
Generate inquiry, inform and educate, introduce

AUDIENCES
Corporate, internal, consumer

LW

What's good about this poster is that it does use the imagery of the Eames', which is by now of course solidly in the design canon, strictly as a point of departure. There's a reference to their work without at all being slavish to it, which makes the interpretation of the subject all the more intriguing. It's wonderful to see a designer not be intimidated by material about other design icons. The poster is a fresh example of using a historical style but developing it in a more contemporary way.

Elika PACKAGING

How do you enhance the three-dimensional qualities of packaging? Make it look as though the box is in shadow.

DESIGNER

Clive Piercy

ART DIRECTORS

Clive Piercy, Michael Hodgson

DESIGN FIRM

Ph.D

CLIENT

Elika

TYPOGRAPHER

Mondo Typo

PRINTER

Crest Paper Box

PAPER

Chipboard

OBJECTIVES

Package/protect, support of sales

AUDIENCES

Corporate, internal, consumer

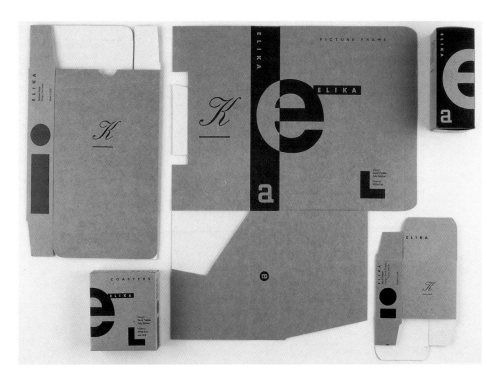

American Center for Design FOURTEENTH ANNUAL **100** SHOW

LW

This fits solidly into a current aesthetic of recycled paper and simplified typography that now operates as a style. It's a revision of minimalism, and is about not expending tremendous amounts of energy or expense in presenting the objects inside the packages. I understand that these packages are for small products that are overtly designed, so therefore it underplays with a typographic cleverness that seems very balanced in this case.

Faith Presbyterian Church STATIONERY

The objective of the Faith Presbyterian Church stationery system was to cause people who had no prior church experience to think about faith in God and to feel welcome attending Faith Presbyterian Church. The typography, vertical background photograph, and colors were developed to emphasize faith in God and a friendly congregation. The typography was hand-ruled into a wordmark reading "Faith". We deliberately kept the words "Faith Presbyterian Church" out of the wordmark in order to focus on Faith. In the wordmark form are two collateral images, the vertical nimbus-like light and a church steeple pointing up to God. The informational typography is set in Optima in all caps and letterspaced to form a platform texture that steps upward. The background photograph of sky and clouds is used to symbolize general Bibical teachings about heaven, peace, God and the return of Jesus Christ. The genuine warmth, approachability and friendliness of the people at Faith Presbyterian Church was expressed using a relaxing blue pastel background color in the printing of the photograph. Raised, warm brown, dull thermography was used for all the typography, implying that there is something real at Faith Presbyterian Church.

DESIGNER
David Kerr

PHOTOGRAPHER
Bruce Law

DESIGN FIRM
Kerr & Company

CLIENT
Faith Presbyterian Church

TYPOGRAPHER
Baseline Type

PRINTER
Gherke

PAPER
Neenah Classic Crest

OBJECTIVE
Introduce

LW

This seemed so strange when I first looked at it. I had to get over the idea of a church developing a logotype and stationery. The more I looked at it, however, the more I realized that it's not corny. It has an imaginative quietude very appropriate for a church. The logo is scaled well. It appears to be ascending and is very airy but not silly looking. It stabilizes how you read it. The color is unexpected. This is all done with a very sure hand and with an innate sense of appropriateness. I wish more institutions that don't normally use image-making actually went this distance.

Guide to Ohio Media Equipment Access Sites

This project required communicating the fact that there are eight media access sites in Ohio that have equipment for sharing or rental. It did not seem appropriate to use visual puns, metaphors, or abstract images; rather, the main elements seemed to be just maps and equipment. Using a video camera, I shot images around Ohio, shot lots of macro views of city maps, and visited access sites to shoot equipment. These were all later input to the Macintosh through a framegrabber board to allow easy access to the images. Alternate meanings to the words "access" and "sites" were overlaid with map and equipment graphics. I also mixed pictures and text on the pages so that each type of information spoke in a different typestyle voice: equipment lists are always sideways; pertinent information is organized along the page edges; redundant boxes are used to highlight information of importance; and so on down the hierarchy of information.

DESIGNER

Crit Warren

EDITOR

Charles G. Fenton

PHOTOGRAPHER

Crit Warren

DESIGN FIRM

Schmeltz + Warren

CLIENT

Ohio Arts Council

PRINTER

Baesman Printing Corp.

PAPER

Warren Patina Matte

OBJECTIVES

Inform and educate

AUDIENCE

Consumer

American Center for Design FOURTEENTH ANNUAL 100 SHOW

LW

The imagery of the equipment and the fuzzy maps make for a wonderful set of images completely appropriate to the twin subjects of this piece: how to get your hands on media equipment and where you might find it. The type is highly articulated, but not overly so. So many pieces that use complex typography for information design wind up being uninformative, but this piece doesn't fall into that trap because it's well organized, both editorially and formally.

ENTRANT'S COMMENTS

This promotional piece for an art school is used as an introduction to the school's programs and application procedures. The cover photography depicts a fast-paced journey from rural settings to the vibrancy of an urban art school. Alternating pages of text provide the "hard" information while the "soft" information of the school's atmosphere and vitality is represented through pages of collaged and vignetted images which offer high school students a glimpse of life at an art school.

DESIGNER
Andrew Blauvelt

DESIGN FIRM
Andrew Blauvelt

CLIENT
Herron School of Art

PRINTER
White Arts

PAPER
Vintage Velvet

OBJECTIVES
Generate inquiry, inform and educate, introduce

AUDIENCES
Internal, consumer

LW

The mysterious photography is a counterpoint to the clarity of the typography. The murky imagery requires the reader to project him or herself into being at that place; an interesting strategy.

American Center for Design FOURTEENTH ANNUAL 100 SHOW

ENTRANT'S COMMENTS

Owned by Britain's Thorn EMI, HMV is the world's largest music retailer with 150 stores worldwide. Their location in Manhattan's upper east side was to be the largest music store in North America. Recognizing the diversity of the New York market, HMV wanted to win over music buyers with its unique store environment and highly personal and knowledgable service approach, which had been its trademark in England and Canada. Frankfurt Gips Balkind was involved in every phase of the HMV campaign, including early research on the US retail, music and video industries and the creation of a promotional kit that introduced HMV to US record distributors. Next came the image campaign, which featured ads in bus shelters and on phone kiosks. To underscore HMV's genuine love of music and depth of selection, visuals included emotional and historical photo images in jazz, classical and rock genres, which were also extended to t-shirts, posters and shopping bags. Image and co-op newspaper advertising and radio spots were also created.

DESIGNER

Johan Vipper

ART DIRECTORS

Kent Hunter, Aubrey Balkind

WRITER

Danny Abelson

ILLUSTRATOR

Herman Leonard

PHOTOGRAPHER

Frederic Lewis

DESIGN FIRM

Frankfurt Gips Balkind

CLIENT

HMV Super Music Stores

TYPOGRAPHER

Frankfurt Gips Balkind

PRINTER

Ambassador Arts

PAPER

Styrene

OBJECTIVES

Introduce, support of sales

AUDIENCE

Consumer

LW

I've seen these on bus shelters in New York, and they look just terrific from the street. The dramatic lighting in the photographs looks great in those bus shelters. The HMV logotype really jumps out at you, even though it's a strange name for a music store.

Hope ADS

ENTRANT'S COMMENTS

The idea of hope and the power of dreaming were the basis for the Oval Room Spring Fashion campaign. Each design becomes the expression of the idea rather than a literal depiction of the clothing.

DESIGNER
Bill Thorburn
WRITER
Alexei Kruchenykh (1913)
PHOTOGRAPHER
Don Freeman
DESIGN FIRM
Dayton Hudson Marshall Field's
CLIENT
Dayton Hudson Marshall Field's
OBJECTIVES
Generate inquiry, inform and educate
AUDIENCE
Consumer

LW

The "not showing the product" strategy taken to the limit. What's really interesting about these is how beautiful and inexplicable they are: just indications of a figure in flowing cloth against backgrounds in which there are fragments of a poem. These are pretty radical in terms of what department stores do to move the spring clothes. While I tend not to be that fond of advertising that sets out to deceive, this is so far gone, so beyond the issue of trying to sell a thing, that it is alluding to spirituality and other qualities you can only hope to pin on a product. When I saw these in magazines I was mesmerized, because they were so different from everything else. The other fashion ad in this show, the Isaac Mizrahi ad chosen by Rick Vermeulen, is fascinating for exactly the opposite reason: it is so explicit that it strips the fashion of its glamour. These ads aren't about glamour, they're about the seduction of a spiritual aesthetic.

Horizon STATIONERY

ENTRANT'S COMMENTS

The Horizon symbol is designed to evoke associations ranging from primitivism to sophistication. The "I" in Horizon relates to the Horizon "eye" and is also intended to emphasize the correct phonetic pronunciation of the word.

DESIGNERS

Clive Piercy, Michael Hodgson

DESIGN FIRM

Ph.D

CLIENT

Horizon Records/A + M Records

PRINTER

Anderson Printing

PAPER

ESSE

OBJECTIVES

Introduce, inform

AUDIENCES

Corporate, internal, consumer

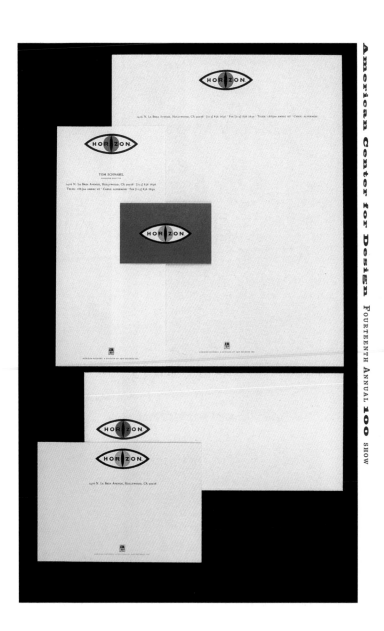

LW

This is a fresh take on one of the great clichés: the single eye used as a hypnotic symbol. There's a wonderful doubling of the iris of the eye standing vertically, turning into the "I" and becoming part of it. The combination of an inventive logo and an elegant and conservative typography is exceptionally pleasing. There's a good use of color, and a thoughtfulness behind the strategy of the elements appearing differently in each piece.

Human Rights Committee BIENNIAL REPORT

ENTRANT'S COMMENTS

This report was commissioned by a nonprofit organization of lawyers who volunteer legal services to victims of torture, and work toward the promotion and protection of human rights worldwide. Our aim, on an uncomfortably snug printing budget, was to present the horror of human rights abuses around the world and highlight the organization's innovative work. We also faced the daunting task of producing a document for attorneys who most appreciate order and consistency in their printed materials. We incorporated odd details to keep readers off balance and to reflect tension and loss-of-control, including hand-rendered text, photographs that were first photocopied and then smeared with Bestine, and copy that, though confined in an attorney-pleasing grid, broke through every so often by jutting into the margin.

DESIGNER
Scott Barsuhn

WRITER
Mary Foster

PHOTOGRAPHER
Magnum/Sigma

DESIGN FIRM
Barsuhn Design

CLIENT
Minnesota Lawyers Human Rights Committee

TYPOGRAPHER
deRuyter-Nelson Publications, Inc.

PRINTER
Kolorpress, Inc.

PAPERS
Productolith Dull, Classic Crest

OBJECTIVES
Inform and educate, document

AUDIENCES
Corporate, consumer

LW

This booklet has a very interesting form. The inside front cover, where the opening statement is handwritten, is mirrored and flopped on the inside left. It's ghostly and disappearing, and is an interesting interpretation of the hidden quality of political aspects of human rights, such as the lack of official acknowledgement and the disappearing. That sort of subtle gesture works very beautifully. The photographs are very dramatic. When the text switches to the hard information of what the organization does, it switches from handwriting to a simple, yet intelligently detailed, san serif type. The whole project is done with imagination, seriousness and intelligence.

Indiana Energy, Inc. 1990 ANNUAL REPORT

ENTRANT'S COMMENTS

Indiana Energy, Inc., is a publicly owned holding company. Its subsidiaries provide local distribution of natural gas to roughly 357,000 customers in Indiana. Featured in the 1990 annual report are stories about IEI customers and their appreciation of natural gas as an energy source. A synthesis of typographic and photographic elements communicate the interdependence of individuals and their natural environment while illustrating everyday uses of natural gas. Panoramic photographs emphasize the platonic quality of the Indiana landscape. Transparency and color interaction suggest the physical interaction of individuals with their environment. Color also highlights relevant information within the customer stories. Uncoated recycled paper appropriately softens the images and further enhances the intended message.

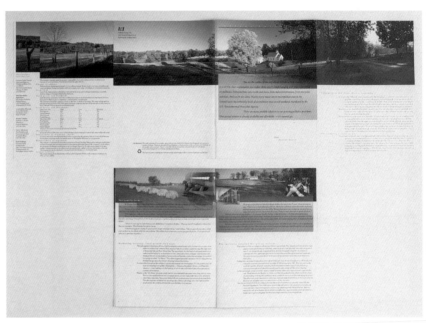

DESIGNERS

Molly Schoenhoff, M. Zender

WRITER

Deborah New

PHOTOGRAPHER

David Steinbrunner/Zender + Associates

DESIGN FIRM

Zender + Associates

CLIENT

Indiana Energy, Inc.

TYPOGRAPHER

Zender + Associates

PRINTER

Central Printing

SEPARATOR

Pam Mar

PAPER

Champion Benefit

OBJECTIVES

Introduce, generate inquiry, inform and educate, document

AUDIENCES

Shareholder, stock analysts

LW

The thing that is so intriguing is the combination of the photographic imagery with a narrative about various uses of energy and various locations. The superimposition of the images is very sophisticated and is knitted in beautifully with the text. An unusually sophisticated use of photography in an annual report.

ENTRANT'S COMMENTS

Komag, the largest independent manufacturer of thin filmed media disks in the world, has entertained a long term relationship with Tolleson Design. This strong foundation has made for fertile ground in terms of meeting the client's creative needs. Because the annual report serves as the company's only marketing piece, Komag sought to convey all aspects of their business: manufacturing, philosophy and technology. Since the book presents a lot of information and highly technical product description, we wanted this annual report to be unintimidating. Lindsay Beaman, a skilled commercial writer, sought to make the editorial light and palettable, while Tolleson Design further communicated the idea through the use of visual typography and imagery. In keeping with previous annual reports that our office has produced for Komag, we featured the media discs on the cover. The large thin numbers were primarily used to identify their different size discs while infusing them with an element of precision. Icons were created to help visually represent certain segments of information that the company wanted to emphasize. Ron Chan's illustrations depict analogies for otherwise inconceivable facts. A double gate fold presents the theme of this year's annual report ("Survival through continuous improvement...Success through innovation") and illustrates their product development.

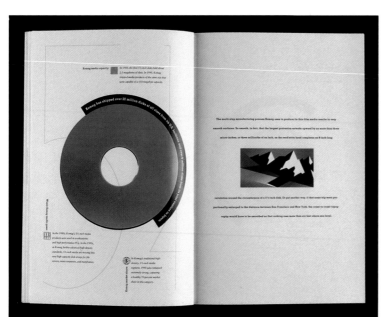

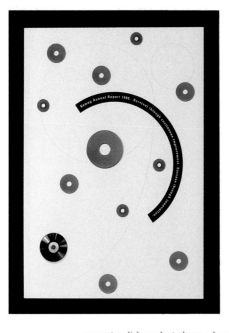

DESIGNERS
Steven Tolleson, Bob Aufuldish

ART DIRECTOR
Steven Tolleson

WRITER
Lindsay Beaman

PHOTOGRAPHER
Henrik Kam

DESIGN FIRM
Tolleson Design

CLIENT
Komag

TYPOGRAPHER
Type Spartan Typographers

PRINTER
Lithographix

SEPARATOR
Lithographix

PAPER
Loe Dull

OBJECTIVES
Inform and educate

AUDIENCE
Shareholders

LW

The pages that illustrate and describe the company's various computer disk products have a beautiful form, with product information super-imposed on the disks through particularly fine typography. They've become beautiful formal compositions which jump beyond the bland imaging you see in most annual reports.

LA Auto Mart

The design objective was to create a logotype that encompassed the spirit and state-of-the-art technology of Southern California auto culture. The logotype has thus far been successfully applied to exterior signage and promotional brochures.

American Center for Design FOURTEENTH ANNUAL 100 SHOW

DESIGNER

Heather Wielandt

ART DIRECTOR

James Cross

WRITER

Julie Wunderlich

DESIGN FIRM

Cross Associates

CLIENT

The Ratkovich Company

TYPOGRAPHER

Central

PRINTER

Platinum Press

SEPARATOR

Platinum Press

PAPER

Reflections

OBJECTIVES

Generate inquiry, introduce

AUDIENCE

Consumer

LW

I'm predisposed to not be particularly interested in work that is very slick, but this piece, which is slicker than slick, is appropriately so. It was created for a real estate development that seeks to put together different auto dealers in a historic renovated space in downtown Los Angeles. The references to automobiles include the slickness and the logotype on the cover, referring to the curves of the car. Vernacular typography is used without the clichés.

Level STATIONERY

Level is a design and build company specializing in interior design and unique interior fittings and furniture. The design for the Level mark intentionally plays against the expectation that the name elicits – cueing the observer that exceptions are as important as expectations. Even the paper surface is not level; it has a debossed band running up the left side. When the sheet is folded, the pyramid of type on the back, "art/craft/design/furniture/environment," meets the triangle on the front, which becomes its crown. Something which at first seemed a purely formal device is connected to, and becomes part of, the explanation of the firm's underlying philosophy. (The words on the back are the thinking behind the process and object; they come to the foreground only when the letter is folded, and recede as the content is considered.) Drawing on the underlying principles of Level's art and craft, the mark itself is an assemblage of typographic furniture, individually crafted letter-forms, which respond to and operate within their own environment or interior space.

DESIGNERS
Brad Collins, Diane Kasprowilz, Gretchen Sloble

ART DIRECTOR
Brad Collins

CLIENT
Level

TYPOGRAPHER
Group C

PRINTER
Camelli Printing

PAPER
Strathmore

LW

There's a very subtle but beautiful interpretation of the notion of aesthetics through construction operating in this design: the subtle colors and the emboss of the mark create a tenuous balance. Even though it's very carefully detailed, it is not overwhelming.

A four-letter word describing what designers sometimes do to themselves and to others, including other designers. At the rate at which we consume ideas, ideals, formal queries and stylistic aberrations, the tenuous sympatico between the message and the voice that makes for communicating, for being heard, is sometimes diminished to a vague whispering or even lost. The reflective and interpretive potential of the designer's efforts have inherent implication inside and outside the visual and intellectual levels of understanding; these implications become affective and determining elements in the texture of one's life, regardless of one's position in the sender-message-receiver spectrum. The voice makes the important difference – as in a numbing, numberless crowd – while the sign, not without complicity, is heard, transferred, and elementally changed.

DESIGNER

Allen Hori

WRITER

with Anne Abele

DESIGN FIRM

Lift

CLIENT

Allen Hori

TYPOGRAPHER

Allen Hori

PRINTER

Vormgeving Rotterdam

OBJECTIVES

Generate inquiry, inform and educate

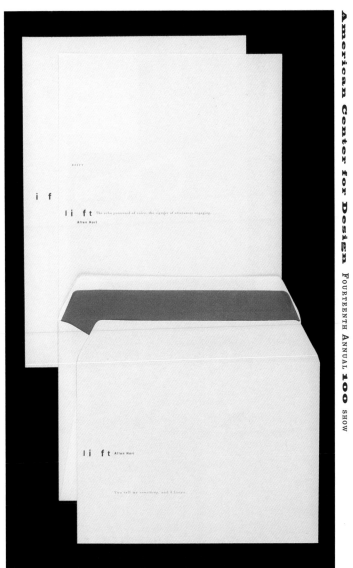

American Center for Design FOURTEENTH ANNUAL 100 SHOW

LW

This is the far edge of poetics applied to graphic design. We don't know the phone number, we don't know the fax; but we do get a clear picture of the designer's passionate and poetic interest in communication. So little information is offered on the stationery, yet the little mottos ("you tell me something and I listen") are completely compelling.

Listen Up: The Lives of Quincy Jones

Frankfurt Gips Balkind created a 192-page coffee table book on Quincy Jones' life as part of a comprehensive marketing program. The book is sold in book and music stores and is packaged with the movie soundtrack and promotional movie poster. The design used emotional, expressive type to engage the MTV generation and music enthusiasts with the copy.

DESIGNERS

Riki Sethiadi, Johan Vipper, Thomas Bricker

ART DIRECTORS

Kent Hunter, Aubrey Balkind

EDITOR

Courtney Sale Ross

DESIGN FIRM

Frankfurt Gips Balkind

CLIENT

Warner Books

TYPOGRAPHER

Frankfurt Gips Balkind

OBJECTIVES

Generate inquiry, inform and educate, document

AUDIENCE

Consumer

LW

Beautiful art direction and incredible use of vintage and contemporary photography. The text of the Quincy Jones quotes is pulled out and turned into animated lines, punctuating and contrasting with the photos. Every page appears to have been designed with the specific text on the page in mind. Gorgeous color and terrific printing for a commercial book.

Mitchell Kane CATALOG

ENTRANT'S COMMENTS

A catalog for a show which surveys the work of a contemporary artist. The traditional catalog has been rendered as a two-sided "map", with one side functioning as a collection of the artist's work and the other as the graphic equivalent of an installation by the artist. The intent was to avoid the typical exhibition catalog and its treatment (reverence) of the art work. The format is a reference to the vernacular travel guides and maps of companies like Fodors. The catalog concept was a collaboration with the artist whose work also makes use of everyday materials and vernacular references.

DESIGNER

Andrew Blauvelt

ART DIRECTORS

Andrew Blauvelt, Mitchell Kane

WRITER

Anne Rorimer

DESIGN FIRM

Andrew Blauvelt

CLIENT

Herron Gallery

PRINTER

White Arts

SEPARATOR

Rheitone

PAPER

Curtis Brightwater, Kromekote

OBJECTIVES

Inform and educate, document

AUDIENCES

Internal, consumer

LW

The format of this catalog is most interesting. It's based on a road atlas, where a folded poster is attached to a booklet cover. It uses this format very cleverly to hold the biography, bibliography, and a catalog of the material. This is a rarely used, relatively inexpensive format. It does seem to bear a close relation to the concerns of the artist, particularly the piece called "The War With Mexico", in which there is an exploration of information and the recording of geographic and historical facts.

The Name Remains the Same

Being a busy freelance designer, I have little time for the things that got me interested in the field in the first place. In making "The Name Remains the Same" I returned to the roots of my love for graphic design: letterpress printing and bookmaking. A project without a deadline, I was able to lavish attention on the details of the design, materials and writing until I was completely satisfied.

DESIGNER

Rebecca Chamlee

WRITER

Rebecca Chamlee

DESIGN FIRM

Rebecca Chamlee Design

CLIENT

Rebecca Chamlee

TYPOGRAPHER

Rebecca Chamlee

PRINTERS

Jean Krikorian, Rebecca Chamlee

PAPERS

Speckletone, Parchkin

OBJECTIVES

Inform and educate

AUDIENCES

Friends and clients

LW

What is so engaging about this piece is the coordination of the design and the writing. (The designer is the writer, so the results are uniquely coherent.) It's amazing that this piece doesn't put the reader off, given that the announcement of a name change is accompanied by this confessional essay that might offend some sensibilities. But the personal history, the way the text works, and the beautiful typography and production transcend self-indulgence to create a strong, self-affirming piece.

New Spanish Painting CATALOG

ENTRANT'S COMMENTS

The design decisions arose from the need for the catalog to be bilingual, the limited printing budget, and the desire to express a sense of Spanish mystique.

DESIGNERS
Judith Lausten, Renee Cossutta

WRITER
Lucinda Barnes

DESIGN FIRM
Lausten/Cossutta Design

CLIENT
University Art Museum,
California State University,
Long Beach

TYPOGRAPHER
Continental Typographers

PRINTER
Donahue Printing, Inc.

PAPER
Speckletone, Mojave Matte

OBJECTIVES
Inform and educate, document

AUDIENCES
Art, academic

LW

A formally beautiful catalog and an exemplary piece of bilingual graphic design. Rather than shoving the interpretations into the back of the book, the texts and even the footnotes are run simultaneously in English and Spanish, accomplished with clarity. It serves as a very interesting model for the kind of project which, at least in many parts of the country, is going to become more common.

Ohio Media Equipment Access POSTER

ENTRANT'S COMMENTS

This media poster was an extension of a page from the Guide to Ohio Media Equipment Access Sites. As with that brochure, it did not seem appropriate to use visual puns, metaphors, or abstract images. Instead, I chose a presentation of a film and video micro/macro map of Ohio. The images were all shot around Ohio with a video camera, and a framegrabber board in a Macintosh let me choose and capture scenes quickly. One-color for economic reasons, I chose a composition that allowed lots of white space to play off the concentrated images for contrast.

DESIGNER
Crit Warren

EDITOR
Charles G. Fenton

PHOTOGRAPHER
Crit Warren

DESIGN FIRM
Schmeltz + Warren

CLIENT
Ohio Arts Council

PRINTER
Baesman Printing Corp.

PAPER
Warren Patine Matte

OBJECTIVES
Inform and educate

AUDIENCE
Consumer

LW

I chose this piece for the same reasons I chose its companion brochure (see p. 37). The imagery is again completely appropriate, and the piece as a whole remains informative in spite of the highly articulated type.

Ostro Design STATIONERY

Seeing yourself clearly and projecting that image is never an easy task. The first objective was to be objective. The second objective was to create an extremely refined and distinguished image, yet one that felt fresh to both the eye and the touch. Ultimately, this image must demonstrate a sensitivity to typography and fine printing techniques (engraving, embossing and offset) and allow for a certain versatility in use. The simplicity and elegance of the letterform O served as a creative springboard. Three different O's were developed in three different colors, each conveying its own distinctive tone yet maintaining a strong unity. It is this aspect which allows for the flexibility of mixing or matching when using the stationery elements. The distinctive O's created the spark of excitment, while the use of old-style engraved typography and the envelope seal grounds the image with a refined, distinguished and professional look.

DESIGNER

Michael Ostro

DESIGN FIRM

Ostro Design

CLIENT

Ostro Design

TYPOGRAPHER

Mono Typesetting

PRINTERS

Swanson Engraving, Briarwood Printing Co.

PAPER

Cranes Crest

OBJECTIVES

Inform and educate, introduce, support of sales

AUDIENCES

Corporate, consumer

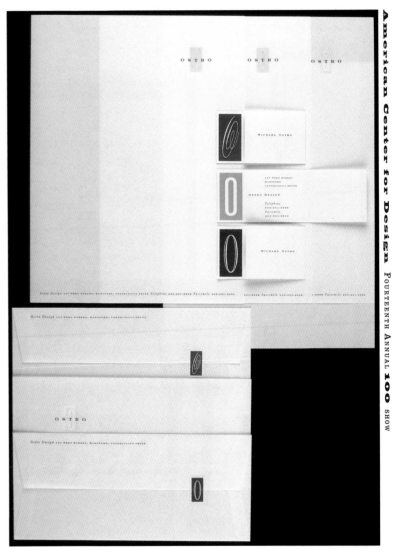

American Center for Design FOURTEENTH ANNUAL 100 SHOW

LW

I responded to the combination of formality and utter looseness in this design. Basically, it looks like the designer solved the dilemma of not knowing which O to use for his initial by using all of them, in lots of favorite colors, even going so far as to emboss many different O's on the letterhead. It's a masterpiece of indecision. And yet it also works together as a kit of parts, a way of changing the way the system is put together each time a letter goes out. Very cleverly done.

Oyster is a free quarterly in Chicago open to any contributor with a provocative thought. This was our first cover, mission statement and first entry by Rick Valicenti, and was a cooperative effort by a writer, designer, architectural team, and advertising agency. The reason for this long term undertaking is to explore and experiment with the process and notion of cooperation.

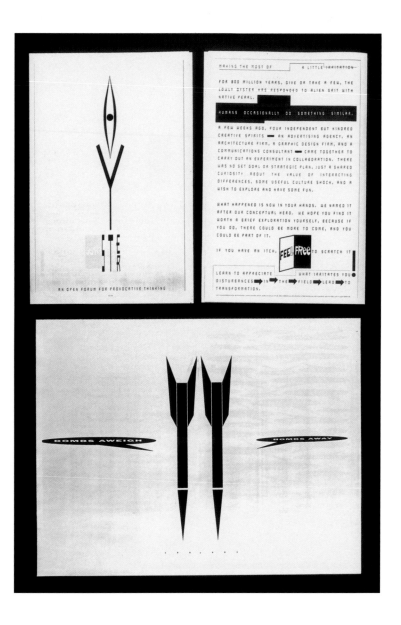

DESIGNER
Rick Valicenti

WRITER
Todd Lief

DESIGN FIRM
Thirst

CLIENT
Self

TYPOGRAPHER
Thirst

PRINTER
Best Web

PAPER
Newsprint

OBJECTIVES
Generate inquiry, inform and educate

AUDIENCE
General public

LW

An encouraging example of another good project initiated by a designer. It's exactly what it says it is: an open journal for provocative thinking, a call for opinions. The typography is provocative; it invites comment. The eccentricity of the typography fits in wonderfully with the intention of the editors, one of whom is of course the designer himself. I'm looking forward to the invited comments.

Reports

The design corroborates a fictional account devised by the author, Dan Hoffman, chair of the Architecture Program at the Cranbrook Academy. The text and photographs take the reader into an ambiguous but believable realm of science and travel. The typography mimics 19th century goverment land surveys, then fuses that to a common-place futuristic aesthetic. The subjective language used to describe what the discoverers find marks a contrast to the approach to data we use today. I hope the design does the same.

DESIGNER

Laurie Haycock Makela

WRITER

Dan Hoffman

DESIGN FIRM

Commbine, Cranbrook

CLIENT

Storefront for Art & Architecture

TYPOGRAPHER

Key Tech

PRINTER

Typocraft

OBJECTIVE

Document

AUDIENCES

Art, architecture, design

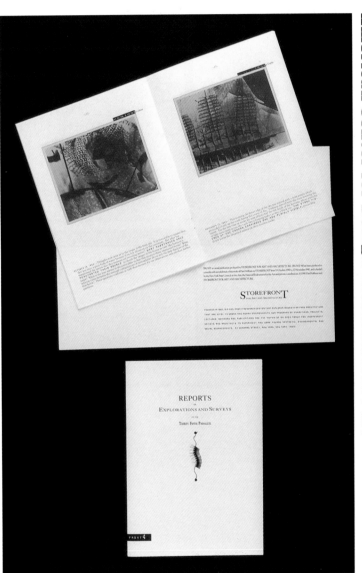

LW

The integrity of this project results from the collaboration between the designer and author, in this case the architect Dan Hoffman. Formally, the piece sits at an interesting crossroad between Victorian scientific positivism, the vernacular of the scientific report played out typographically, and the use of photographs and a measurement dating system that looks like it comes out of satellite photography. The whole piece speaks poetically and comes out of the obvious symbiosis of the aims of the author and the designer.

Seagrams 1991 Annual Report

Seagrams wanted this report to illustrate how its employees were contributing to the realization of its corporate mission. Since that mission is a living, evolving goal, open-ended discussions with employees were conducted. The themes which emerged were divided into six pairs of seemingly opposing concepts. All told, fifty-seven Seagrams employees from around the world appear in the report.

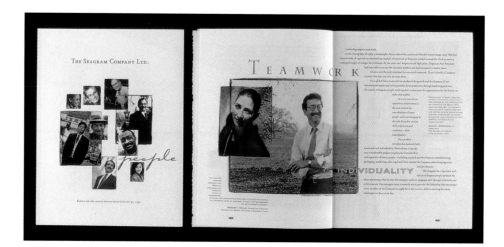

DESIGNER

Benjamin Bailey

ART DIRECTOR

Kent Hunter

WRITER

Bob Kasmire

PRODUCT PHOTOGRAPHER

Doug Whyte

PORTRAIT PHOTOGRAPHER

Daniel Borris

DESIGN FIRM

Frankfurt Gips Balkind

CLIENT

Seagrams Co., Ltd.

TYPOGRAPHER

Frankfurt Gips Balkind

PRINTER

Arthurs-Jones Lithography

PAPERS

Strathmore Pastel Natural, White Renewal, Fluorescent White

OBJECTIVES

Generate inquiry, inform and educate, support of sales, document

AUDIENCES

Corporate, internal, consumer, shareholder

LW

The front of this annual report uses the very familiar strategy of a series of interviews with employees, showing off the human resources of the company. The formal quality of this book is so stunning, however, that it takes this ordinary approach and makes it very special. There's a graceful use of layered photography, which allows you to actually see through transparent images to other images. They're very casual portraits, which are contrasted with an extraordinarily detailed and fussy typography which pulls you in through the beauty of the details. There's a playful use of headline faces that connect to the traditional trademark typographic forms that you see on the labels of beverages. In addition, the designers use a blind emboss which also refers to the labels. The overall effect of the report is extremely decorative, but the references engage the reader into the text; it is not just silly complexity. The printing of this complex piece is extraordinary as well.

Skolos/Wedell STATIONERY

The Skolos/Wedell identity was designed to reflect the spirit of our studio's design and photography. The logo plays on ambiguity between two and three dimensions which is one of our particular interests. Embossed areas are used to reference the photographic designs we create with three dimensional constructions. Woodgrain is an element on the stationery that represents one of the many textures we incorporate in our constructions. The two-color, embossed design was generated on the Macintosh using Aldus FreeHand. Its expensive appearance has been criticized for being too extravagant. The stationery, however, has become an extremely useful promotional piece that was well worth the investment.

DESIGNER

Nancy Skolos

DESIGN FIRM

Skolos/Wedell

CLIENT

Skolos/Wedell

PRINTER

Reynolds-DeWalt Printing

PAPER

Mohawk Poseidon White Smooth

OBJECTIVE

Support of sales

AUDIENCE

Corporate

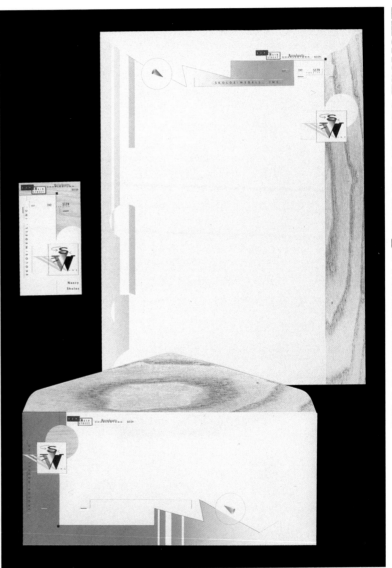

American Center for Design FOURTEENTH ANNUAL 100 SHOW

LW

This appears to be a kind of end-point of complexity, an ultimate neo-constructivist, neo-everything rolled into one. It teeters and falls over the edge of overdoneness, but in such a wonderfully crafted way that one can't help but laugh. I believe that the humor *is* intentional: the purple-y wood grain on the flap of the envelope, the little embossed squares frantically zipping all over it. In its excess, it's a very funny piece.

Spring Festival POSTER

This poster and program cover, directed to parent audiences, use typographic form and imagery that allude to inheritance and the genetic code in celebration of springtime performances. The strand of genetic material, DNA, symbolizes the notion that a child's ability to perform can be attributed in part to the parents' own springtime activities. The rhythmic DNA strand also serves as strings on which two bows ride, visually linking science and music. Petri-like plates, hinting at concepts of birth and growth, become anchors for a typographic configuration resembling the "X" shape of a chromosome. As this project is directed to a specific, well-educated audience, I felt comfortable offering more involved analogies. In addition, I took advantage of the opportunity to explore aspects of type design outside the restrictive boundaries of "commercial" graphic design.

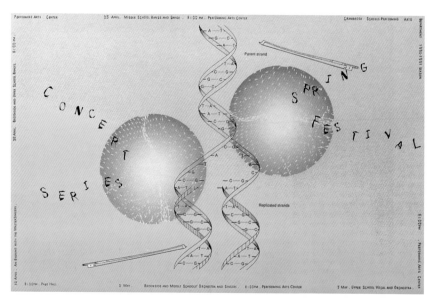

DESIGNER
Lisa Langhoff

DESIGN FIRM
One Good Dog

CLIENT
Cranbrook Schools Performing Arts

PRINTER
Lessnav Printers

OBJECTIVES
Generate inquiry, inform

AUDIENCES
Internal, parents of grade school and middle school children

LW

Combining biological imagery (particularly the unravelling strands of DNA) with imagery for a spring music festival at a grade school and middle school is a pretty funny conceptual leap, something that pulls in the parents, the sunny and celestial image of genetics, and the music. The bows from the violin reaching toward the DNA also works very well.

A Surprise Inside! CATALOG

ENTRANT'S COMMENTS

This project was born when the editor and designer were sharing a box of Cracker Jack and discussing popular culture at a Phillies baseball game. The subject of the exhibition, John Walworth, designs pop-up paper and plastic gizmos found at the bottom of Cracker Jack and cereal boxes. Walworth had saved samples of everything he had designed. This catalog documents the exhibition and Walworth's accomplishments. The objects in the exhibition are found at the bottom of boxes after digging through the contents. Carothers created the same feeling by thinking of the catalog as a box of Cracker Jack/cereal, the text as the caramel popcorn/cereal, and the images as the prize found among the contents. Walworth used a simple rivet to create dials. Carothers designed the catalog cover as the ultimate Walworth dial. Most of Walworth's work is printed using the four process colors as flat colors or with simple overprinting and screens to create secondary colors. Carothers incorporated this aspect into the headings, folios, captions and page accents.

DESIGNER
Martha Carothers

WRITER
Belena Chapp

PHOTOGRAPHERS
Kathleen Clark, Peter Croydon, Raymond Nichols, Bob Herbert

ILLUSTRATOR
John Walworth

DESIGN FIRM
The Post Press

CLIENT
University Gallery, University of Delware

TYPOGRAPHER
Graphic Communications Center

PRINTER
Cedar Tree Press

PAPER
Mohawk

OBJECTIVES
Inform and educate, document

AUDIENCE
Consumer

LW

This is just a wonderful little book. Rather than falling into a cute recreation of the obvious kitsch elements of Walworth's work, it instead offers a lightness and humor in the choice of types and heads, without actually mimicking the premiums themselves or the graphics that came with them. It's a wonderful project, and the designer's efforts to help characterize this curious pop culture character are quite well done.

Tactics of Posture POSTER

This poster served to promote a series of lectures by contemporary artists who make reference to the human body in their work. The poster's imagery refers to the historical evolution of the human body from a microcosmic and all encompassing entity to its fragmentation through dissection and decapitation. The design seeks to provide background "information" to potential attendees about the theme of the lecture series rather than depicting each artist's work.

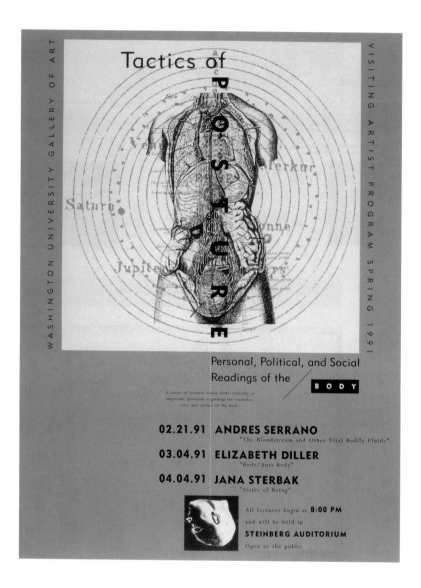

DESIGNER

Andrew Blauvelt

WRITER

Christopher Scoates

DESIGN FIRM

Andrew Blauvelt

CLIENT

Washington University Gallery of Art

PRINTER

White Arts

PAPER

Productolith

OBJECTIVES

Generate inquiry, inform and educate

AUDIENCES

Consumer, internal

LW

I responded to the unity of this poster's structure: the rigid center axis, the placement of the word "posture" through the spine of the old anatomical drawing and then through the center of the universe, the lining up of the type underneath. There are so many things about this poster that aren't particularly compelling, like the clumsy-ish typography or the color, but it appeared so strong among the group of posters entered precisely because of the tight alignment of the poster's basic composition and the subject matter of the lecture series that it's describing. It's a very intelligent and appropriate piece.

Time Warner Logo

ENTRANT'S COMMENTS

Warner is primarily entertainment; Time is essentially journalism. A common denominator needed to be much broader: looking and listening, reading, receiving and sending. That's really the essence of communications. Time Warner's products appeal to the eye and ear.

DESIGNER

Steff Geissbuhler

DESIGN FIRM

Chermayeff & Geismar Inc.

CLIENT

Time Warner

OBJECTIVE

Identify

AUDIENCE

Corporate

American Center for Design FOURTEENTH ANNUAL 100 SHOW

LW

All those books published in the past few years on American and European logotypes of the 1920s and 1930s have obviously affected recent symbol design. This logotype is an excellent example of the contemporary tendency toward more literal or pictorial logo design, even when the client is an abstract organization such as a large multinational corporation.

An Installation on Transparency
INVITATION & BROCHURE

The series consists of an announcement and brochure documentation for an installation and exhibition of work by the designer at the University of Akron Emily Davis Gallery in Spring 1990. The announcement, printed on vellum, makes obvious reference to the theme being explored: transparency. Text and typographic elements are further utilized as fragmented parts, in various stages of layout. The brochure serves as the documentation for the temporary installation, with an outer shell of vellum serving as an encasing element, very similar to the installation created by the designer, in which the theme of transparency is explored both literally and mentally as a way of working and thinking.

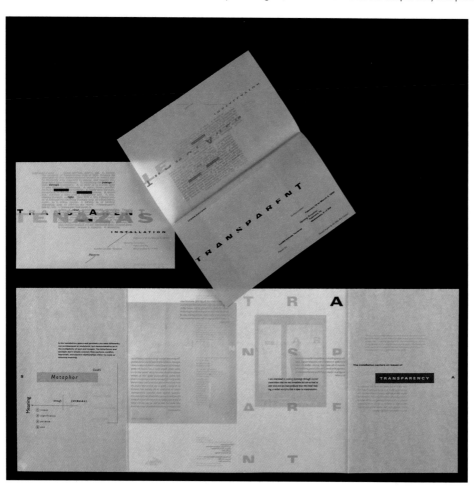

DESIGNER

Lucille Tenazas

WRITERS

Lucille Tenazas, Deborah Ramage

PHOTOGRAPHER

Richard Barnes

DESIGN FIRM

Tenazas Design

CLIENT

University of Akron Emily Davis Gallery

TYPOGRAPHER

Ken Rackow

PRINTER

Techni-Graphics

SEPARATOR

Techni-Graphics

PAPERS

Invitation: UV Ultra
Brochure: Curtis Parchment

OBJECTIVES

Generate inquiry, inform and educate

AUDIENCE

Design community

LW

This is another example of a project initiated by a designer. The designer produced these pieces as an adjunct to an installation in a gallery in which she uses the physical and visual phenomenon of transparency as a metaphor for change. These pieces employ a strong typographic exploration of this phenomenon which is aided by a dissection of meaning. It all works together very harmoniously.

Typography in Asia: A View from Tokyo

"Typography in Asia: A View from Tokyo" was published to celebrate a collaborative exhibition between The Cooper Union School of Art in New York City and the Toyo Institute of Art and Design in Tokyo. The design of the catalog was strongly influenced by my trip to Japan as a guest lecturer at the Toyo Institute. Many perceptions of the visual world were altered: space became form, fragility became strength, and dream became reality. The catalog design reflects these transpositions. Whiteness (space) becomes the dominant visual element of the page. In sharp contrast to its more traditional role as margin or border, it is not subservient to text or image (form). Columns of text are weightless, suspended from an invisible horizontal thread (fragility). The multi-lingual text cannot be deciphered with a glance, but demands thoughtful contemplation (strength). Images, manuscripts, and memories from many parts of the world float on the surface of my table (dream). I guide them to their place (reality).

DESIGNER
Margaret Morton

EDITOR
Ellen Lupton

DESIGN FIRM
Margaret Morton Designer

CLIENT
The Cooper Union

TYPOGRAPHER
The Cooper Union, Off Typo, Inc.

PRINTER
Red Ink Productions

PAPER
FrostBright Matte

OBJECTIVES
Inform and educate, document

AUDIENCES
General public, design community

LW

This book and the Bauhaus book were issued by the Herb Lubalin Center for the Study of Design and Typography, and are superior for similar reasons. It's not that they are groundbreaking in formal terms. What is interesting is the involvement of graphic designers in the publishing, editing and production of these very serious research pieces on subjects connected to graphic design. These efforts are really quite important. "Typography in Asia" combines multi-lingual typography, made even more difficult by a non-Western alphabet, and evolves it quite clearly. This is a situation where a layout has to be exceedingly organized. The Herb Lubalin Study Center has to be lauded for these projects.

ENTRANT'S COMMENTS

One day, I found an option in the FreeHand program that automatically stacks type vertically. Kathy Halbreich, the new director at the Walker, initially rejected the piece, saying simply, "It's inscrutable." Convinced it was a beautiful puzzle – the student who solved it gets the job – I was reluctant to let it go. Instead I added the column on the right. The results may be a nice polemic about the poetic and the practical. The guy who got the job said the thing he didn't like about the piece was the column on the right.

THE WALKER ART CENTER, A MUSEUM OF CONTEMPORARY ART, OFFERS A TWELVE-MONTH DESIGN INTERNSHIP THAT IS A FULL-TIME POSITION IN THE GRAPHIC DESIGN DEPARTMENT. THE INTERN WILL ASSIST IN DESIGNING EXHIBITION PUBLICATIONS, SIGNAGE, POSTERS AND BROCHURES FOR THE WALKER'S MUSIC, DANCE, FILM, THEATER, AND EDUCATION PROGRAMS. INDIVIDUALS WITH A BFA OR AN MFA DEGREE IN DESIGN ARE INVITED TO APPLY BY JUNE 7, 1991. A STIPEND OF $13,000 WILL BE OFFERED. INTERNSHIP BEGINS ON SEPTEMBER 1, 1991 AND CONCLUDES ON AUGUST 30, 1992. PLEASE SUBMIT A RESUME OR LETTER, 10 SLIDES, NAMES OF TWO REFERENCES, AND A STAMPED ENVELOPE FOR THE RETURN OF SLIDES TO DESIGN DEPARTMENT WALKER ART CENTER VINELAND PLACE MINNEAPOLIS MN 55403 AA/EOE/W/M/H

1991–1992
Walker ART
CENTER

Design Internship

DESIGNER
Laurie Haycock Makela

CLIENT
Walker Art Center

PAPER
Carnival Groove

OBJECTIVE
Generate inquiry

AUDIENCE
Design students

LW

This is one of those pieces that seems to me to be telling us where we or some of us might end up going next. It's a very, very strange poster. The complexity of it comes from this simple demonstration of how we can read and how we can't read. It gives you the alternative of either walking through the piece, or crawling through it. It has all sorts of interesting resonances between demonstrating the most simple versus the most completely arcane manners of reading. It also really talks about just how hard and/or how easy the designer can make life for everybody else. And it does all this with a tiny expenditure of energy: just one color of ink.

Srubas/Giammanco Wedding Invitation

ENTRANT'S COMMENTS

With this wedding invitation, we tried to tell our families and friends how we felt about the event. We wanted the piece to be elegant and festive, with a bit of humor. Our choices of paper, color, and letterpress gave it a sensual quality. The design is part of a long collaboration.

DESIGNERS
Amy Srubas, Michael Giammanco

WRITERS
Amy Srubas, Michael Giammanco

PRINTER
Julie Holcomb

PAPER
Rieves BFK

OBJECTIVE
Inform

AUDIENCES
Friends, family

LW

It is very beautiful, in the way that wedding invitations should be, but it adds a sense of humor to the traditional form. The exaggerated engraving behind the type is a wonderful gesture. The typography is very formal, but not quite "correct". It's joyous without being pretentious, yet it plays with the stiff conventions at the same time. The superb letterpress printing and beautiful materials harken back to the properly printed wedding invitations of years ago (the kind hardly anyone does anymore).

World Heavyweight Championship
SOUVENIR PROGRAM

ENTRANT'S COMMENTS

Hal Riney & Partners, a San Francisco based advertising agency working with the Mirage Hotel in Las Vegas, asked Pentagram to design a souvenir program to commemorate the championship fight between Buster Douglas and Evander Holyfield which was held at the Mirage Hotel in the Fall of 1990.

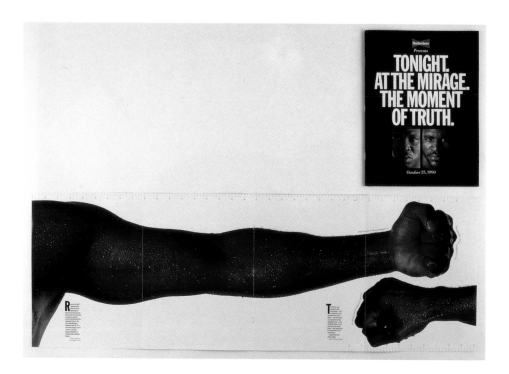

DESIGNER

Neil Shakery

ART DIRECTOR

Ben Wong

WRITER

Sam Pond

PHOTOGRAPHER

Robert Mizzone

DESIGN FIRM

Pentagram

CLIENT

The Mirage Hotel

TYPOGRAPHER

Omnicomp

PRINTER

Woods Litho

SEPARATOR

Woods Litho

PAPER

Quintessence

AUDIENCE

Consumer

LW

A classic piece of information design disguised as commercial hype. It's a complete visual surprise to see things like Holyfield's arms at full size. It's dramatic and funny. You don't expect to see body parts reproduced to scale along with the rulers to measure them by. It's done so well that it doesn't even matter that it's only a beer promotion.

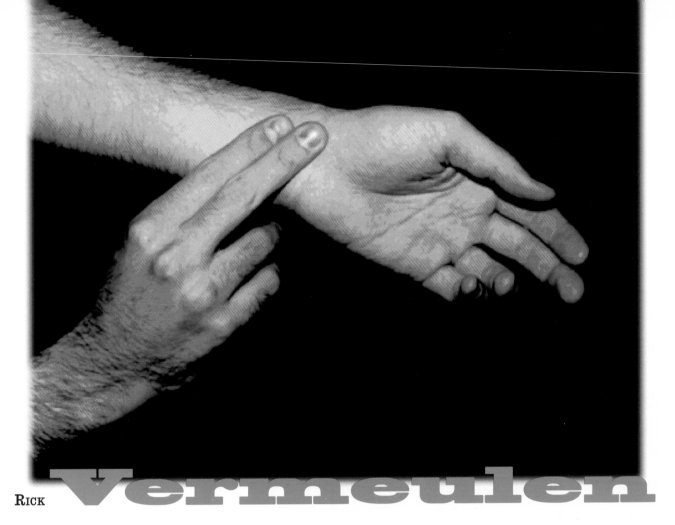

SELECTIONS

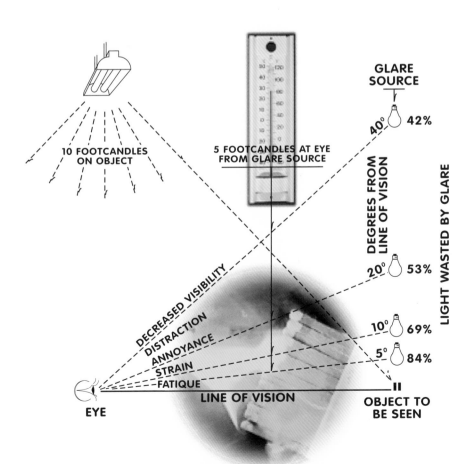

GLARE
SOURCE

10 FOOTCANDLES
ON OBJECT

5 FOOTCANDLES AT EYE
FROM GLARE SOURCE

40° 42%

DEGREES FROM
LINE OF VISION

LIGHT WASTED BY GLARE

20° 53%

DECREASED VISIBILITY

DISTRACTION

ANNOYANCE

10° 69%

5° 84%

STRAIN

FATIQUE

LINE OF VISION

EYE

OBJECT TO
BE SEEN

ENTRANT'S COMMENTS

The Hallmark Visiting Educators Program is an annual event in which educators nationwide are flown to the headquarters of Hallmark Cards, Inc. The instructors tour various creative departments to learn more about the company. This promotional piece was designed to represent a few of the functions of the Package Design department and also serve as a momento of the program. The record incorporates various packaging components: label, hangtag, surface design, and structure. The piece also emphasizes the highest of packaging concerns – communication. Environmental issues are addressed in a unique manner by utilizing a recycled lunch tray as a backing. Graphic references to travel serve as reminders of the journey and allude to the title of the song "Kansas City".

DESIGNERS
Anne Van Rossum, Sal Costello
ART DIRECTOR
Anne Van Rossum
WRITERS
Anne Van Rossum, Sal Costello
DESIGN FIRM
Hallmark Package Design
CLIENT
Hallmark
PAPER
Recycled lunch trays
OBJECTIVES
Generate inquiry, inform and educate, introduce
AUDIENCE
Visiting educators

RV

It's a great idea for a card company to use a record for a promotional piece. It's humorous, and it's different.

This "radial flow chart" was designed to show in a graphic and engaging way the programs offered by the five schools that constitute California Institute of Arts. Because each school had to be treated with equal importance, a non-linear radial hierarchy was an appropriate solution. The CalArts microcosm can be recognized as part of a greater network. Spores, also microcosms, spin off into space from the parent organism.

DESIGNER

Somi Kim

ILLUSTRATOR

Somi Kim

CLIENT

CalArts

OBJECTIVES

Inform and educate, introduce

AUDIENCES

Prospective students and their parents

American Center for Design FOURTEENTH ANNUAL **100** SHOW

RV

This card explains how this school is organized in a very clear and playful way. The connections between the different disciplines refer to the nucleus of the chemistry model.

ENTRANT'S COMMENTS

Our assignment was to create a newsletter and schedule of events for a museum dedicated to the history of film and video. All images are supplied to us, and consist mostly of movie stills. The challenge is to create a program guide that is simple and legible for easy reference, while being dynamic enough to impart a sense of excitement and movement, all on a tight budget. Most newsletters we've seen are around 8-1/2" x 11" or 8-1/2" x 14" with about 8 pages. This format uses pages folded down to 6" x 8-1/2", yielding between 16 and 24 pages for each newsletter. The smaller format with more pages enables us to pace the booklet in the style of a magazine, with separate sections for exhibitions, listings, museum information, etc.

DESIGNER

Barbera Sullivan

ART DIRECTOR

Alexander Isley

EDITOR

David Draigh

DESIGN FIRM

Alexander Isley Design

CLIENT

American Museum of the Moving Image

TYPOGRAPHER

Natasha Lessnik

PRINTER

Hudson Printing

PAPER

Hammermill

OBJECTIVES

Inform and educate, intriduce, document

AUDIENCE

Consumer

RV

It's a rip-off of a TV or radio guide. Everybody knows how to read and use one. The format allows you to communicate quickly. This extends the idea and it works.

The Big A POSTER

This poster was specifically designed to promote the inexpensive aspect of Ambassador Arts's silk-screening capabilities. Hence the line, "Maximum impact, minimum price."

DESIGNER

Paula Scher

ILLUSTRATOR

Paula Scher

DESIGN FIRM

Pentagram

CLIENT

Ambassador Arts

TYPOGRAPHER

Paula Scher

PRINTER

Ambassador Arts

PAPER

Newsprint

OBJECTIVE

Promotion

AUDIENCES

Corporate, consumer

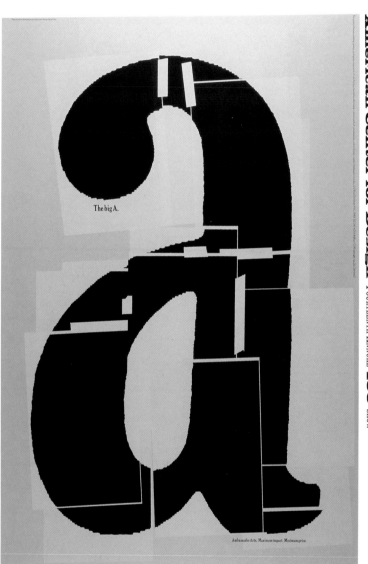

The big A.

Ambassador Arts. Maximum impact. Minimum price.

RV

The silk-screening process is completely reflected in this poster: sticking films together. It doesn't need the text, however. The letterform by itself would be more mysterious and communicative.

American Center for Design FOURTEENTH ANNUAL 100 SHOW

Bowden/Kellett STATIONERY

Bowden/Kellett is a marketing design firm specializing in creative design oriented solutions to marketing problems. I was asked to design for them an identity package that "shows off" their personal and creative approach to problem solving, but without stepping over the line into trendy or faddish decorative trappings. The solution we derived was a typographic design that utilized the unique qualities of offset printing by using both sides of the sheet of paper and taking advantage of the ghost image that normally appears on the other side of the sheet. To enhance the effect (usually considered "bad" or "inferior" printing quality) we selected a very cheap paper with terrible opacity. The result was typography that could be read through the front of the sheet or envelope. The colors selected matched the carefully chosen "corporate" colors of Bowden/Kellett's office interior. The card was printed on UV Ultra, which has transparent attributes and a better tensile strength than the other stock we were working with. The grey version of the design is for copying and faxing where the type must remain intact. And the mailing label (of course) is simply printed on one side. The second sheets are printed on the back only.

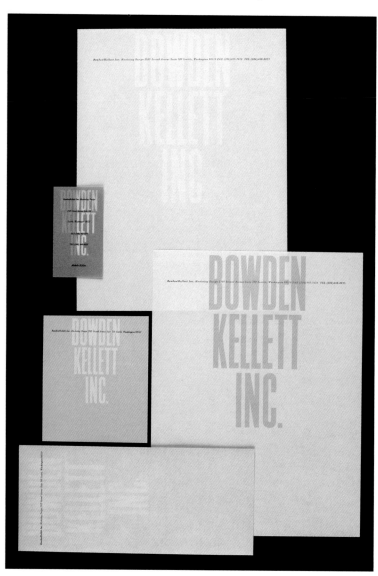

DESIGNER
Art Chantry

ART DIRECTOR
Michele Kellett

DESIGN FIRM
Art Chantry Design

CLIENT
Bowden/Kellett Inc.

TYPOGRAPHER
Rockettype

OBJECTIVES
Introduce, support of sales

AUDIENCE
Corporate

RV

What is attractive here is the obvious: the back printing. I'm most taken by the execution of the envelope; it's the special piece in the whole system. At first it looks like the outside is printed in light grey, but when you open it the surprise comes.

ENTRANT'S COMMENTS

The various clients for this project wanted something on the one hand very traditional (large photos, large type for heads and subheads) and on the other hand not traditional (lots of color, should reflect the school's position of being on the cutting edge), all on a reduced budget. What we came up with is something traditional, expressed exuberantly. The page layout uses a simple two and three column grid with hairline rules, centered heads and subheads in all caps. This was offset by colored pages which distinguish various sections of the catalog. A diminuendo type treatment was also used, which was exaggerated with varying sizes throughout the catalog. The typeface, Hard Times, like the rest of the catalog, takes the traditional or classical (Times Roman), and reworks it for today. This catalog typifies the postmodern approach: not an imitation of earlier models but a re-working or re-consideration of them. Most atypical, however, is the fact that, except for the color, most of the design ideas used are pre-modern.

DESIGNERS

Jeffery Keedy, Edward Fella, Lorraine Wild, P. Lyn Middleton

PHOTOGRAPHER

Steven A. Gunther

CLIENT

CalArts

PRINTER

Donahue Printing, LA

OBJECTIVES

Inform and educate, introduce

AUDIENCES

Prospective students and their parents

RV

I got tricked at first by this piece. I had the impression that everything was printed on different kinds of colored paper, but they are printed four color process. A simple and intelligent idea. The way that the photographs have been treated is also wonderful. I generally like halftones better. The combination of the halftones on a strong flat color is striking, not to mention the title pages, on which the type changes gradually from larger to smaller sizes.

The participants of this music festival in Holland presented an eclectic array of forms of music and performance involving both wide overlaps as well as wide divisions in avant garde music typology. The poster announcing the event takes its character from the program's intention: improvisation, overlap and opposition. An obscenely simple diagram of dissemination – of information, of sound, general to specific, large to small, performer to audience, cohesive to fractured – provides the overall working structure. The slices that occur through the boxes and text work with and against the organizing force of the boxes while not totally eliminating the legibility of the text. These slices were meant to be felt more than seen, as a secondary rhythm; the "divisions" this time providing the "overlap".

DESIGNER
Allen Hori

DESIGN FIRM
Studio Dumbar

CLIENT
Ooyevaer Desk

TYPOGRAPHER
Allen Hori

PRINTER
Imaba Zeeforuk

OBJECTIVES
Generate inquiry, inform and educate

AUDIENCES
Internal, consumer

RV

It's not a street poster; it has an agenda and it works like a charm. Because the festival deals in contemporary music, I think he's succeeded in giving you back improvised stuff. It's well thought out, but it has the quality of improvised music as well.

Columbia Film View MAGAZINE

The assignment was to design a film review magazine. The purpose was to utilize type in the context of editorals as an integrated visual form to enrich the articles and create added interest. Why? Why not! The sky's the limit when there's no interference from MBAs or other middle management in the process.

DESIGNERS
Haggai Shamir, Frederun Scholz

EDITORS
Allison Brandin, Ilana Shulman

PHOTOGRAPHER
Ruggero Gabbai

DESIGN FIRM
Design Provisions

CLIENT
Columbia University

TYPOGRAPHER
Sorel Husbands

AUDIENCE
Consumer

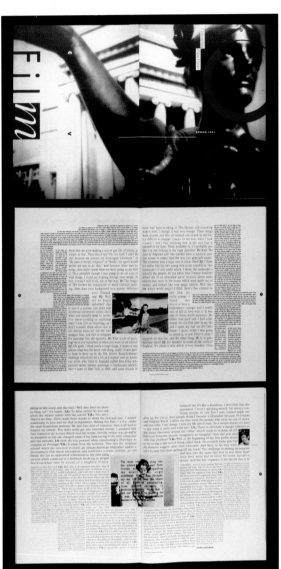

American Center for Design FOURTEENTH ANNUAL 100 SHOW

RV

There is something wonderful about this relatively cheaply produced magazine. Some of the spreads are beautiful. A good effort.

The Conscience of the Eye Dust Jacket

ENTRANT'S COMMENTS

This book examines the relationships between people and cities, and how the latter are designed by the former. Given that many time periods were discussed, it seemed appropriate to depict one era colliding with another. I did the front first, which was unanimously approved; and then I proceeded to do the back, which I immediately recognized to be far stronger. Too late.

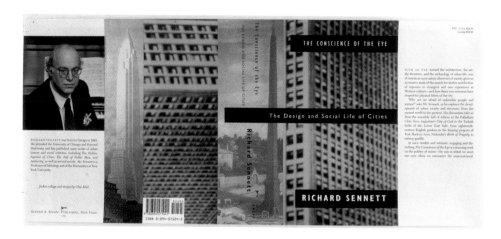

DESIGNER

Chip Kidd

ART DIRECTOR

Carol Devine Carson

WRITER

Richard Sennett

ILLUSTRATOR

Chip Kidd

CLIENT

Alfred A. Knopf, Inc.

TYPOGRAPHERS

C. Kidd, Photolettering

PRINTER

Coral Graphics

SEPARATOR

Coral Graphics

PAPER

Champion White

OBJECTIVE

To visually represent the concept of the text

AUDIENCE

Consumer

RV

There's a great choice and treatment of images here. I like the way they shift and eventually fall together, and how some of the colors are reduced for optimum effect.

ENTRANT'S COMMENTS

Our intent was to help Gilbert Paper show printers and designers that their recycled papers could perform under all conditions. Publications of this type have made similar claims through similar demonstrations. The territory was too familiar to play by the same game plan. Our book was found in the almost predictable headline collection coupled with the unpredictable yet accessible appearance of the RECYCLED mask. The face (made of letters spelling RECYCLED) recycled the German Expressionist approach to type/icon.

DESIGNERS

Rick Valicenti, Michael Giammanco

ART DIRECTOR

Rick Valicenti

WRITER

Michael Giammanco

PHOTOGRAPHER

Corinne Pfister

DESIGN FIRM

Thirst

CLIENT

Gilbert Paper Company

PRINTER

TCR Graphics

TYPOGRAPHER

Thirst

WOODCUT

Tony Klassen

OBJECTIVES

Inform and educate

AUDIENCES

Printers, designers

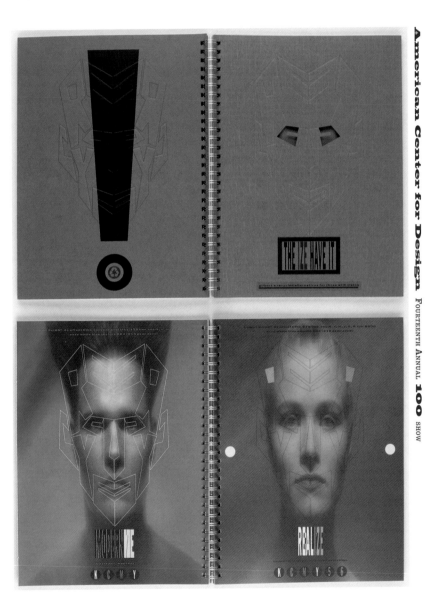

American Center for Design FOURTEENTH ANNUAL **100** SHOW

RV

Paper promotions are great projects to do, since paper manufacturers like to show all the possibilities of their product. The designer created a very intelligent piece for this client. It is, however, a bit dualistic. All this wonderful imagery on various kinds of recycled paper makes you wonder.

ENTRANT'S COMMENTS

Because 1990 was a recession year, it was of particular importance that the tone of the annual report be positive, direct and budget-conscious. This goal was achieved through the design by using 35mm black and white photography with a photo-journalistic quality. The photographs emphasize customer service and show crowded, busy stores. The narrative text was pared down to photo captions, and uncoated recycled paper was used as the printing stock. We want the annual report to have a raw, honest quality in keeping with the times and with Hechinger's reputation as a retailer providing quality products and services at the best prices.

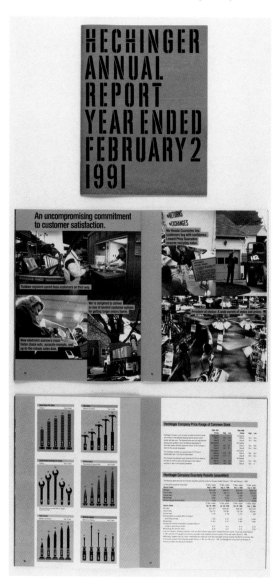

DESIGNER

Bill Anton

PHOTOGRAPHER

Judy Olausen

DESIGN FIRM

Chermayeff & Geismar Inc.

CLIENT

Hechinger Co.

TYPOGRAPHER

New Age

PRINTER

Miocraft

PAPER

Proterra

OBJECTIVES

Inform and educate, document

AUDIENCES

Corporate, internal, shareholder

RV

The design shows the character of the company and their products and services through the choice of imagery, the use of rough paper and two color printing. I'm particularly attracted to the spread with the graphs.

Holidays Record PROMOTIONAL POSTERS

The Holidays are a poppy upbeat modern rock and roll combo preaching a philosophy of "life is wonderful", etc. (Their records are festooned with dayglo mid-1960s daisies and their record company was named after their cat!) with the release of their new record "Every Day is a Holiday", they asked me to come up with a promotional idea that could be used to grab attention on the street as well as in record stores and major-label executive offices. My idea was so simple that it was almost readymade – practically pure concept. There is a company in Arkansas that prints carnival posters (for those small carnivals that tour shopping mall parking lots and the like).

They have stock silkscreened images on otherwise blank board warehoused. A carnival places an order, sends a schedule, and the company returns a series of posters with the image of their choice sporting the various dates on the tour letterpressed in red ink. (Black costs extra!) The wood type they use has had way too many years of use. The result of period images and cracked and chipped letterpressed red type is a dented purity that I would never have been able to duplicate. So I simply ordered a set of posters with identical copy – a simple promotional statement – and asked the printer to mix up the stock images depending on availability. The resulting poster series carries such a cheerful homily demeanor that it proved to be an immediate hit. It currently adorns many record companies' executive suites, and the record is selling quite well, I'll have you know. Oh, and the unit cost was under 50 cents apiece.

DESIGNER

Art Chantry

DESIGN FIRM

Art Chantry Design

CLIENT

Chuckie-Boy Records

TYPOGRAPHER

Neal Walters

PRINTER

Poster Corp.

OBJECTIVES

Introduce, support of sales

AUDIENCES

Internal, consumer

American Center for Design FOURTEENTH ANNUAL **100** SHOW

RV

These are not rock posters, they're circus posters, but they're rock posters. You can use imagery which is familiar to say something else and make the message more interesting. I also like the cheap and simple approach and the idea of making six different posters for one client.

ENTRANT'S COMMENTS

I receive promotional pieces every day. Most I throw out, but the few that I find interesting, beautiful, funny or intriguing I hang on the wall around my workspace for inspiration. We wanted designers, creative directors, editors, art buyers and everybody else to hang Kenneth Willardt's postcards on their walls – and they did.

DESIGNER
Rie Norregaard

ART DIRECTOR
Rie Norregaard

PHOTOGRAPHER
Kenneth Willardt

DESIGN FIRM
Images & Attitudes

CLIENT
Kenneth Willardt

OBJECTIVES
Generate inquiry, introduce

AUDIENCES
Art directors, designers, art buyers

RV

These cards look like they're a joke, but I don't believe they are. There is a second thought to it, which is one of the reasons it attracted me. It's weird, humorous, corny stuff.

Los Angeles Contemporary Exhibitions is an arts organization dedicated to supporting experimental, avant garde and emerging artists. This bias was also extended to the design for LACE under the directorship of Joy Silverman. It is rare that the same autonomy of free expression that is expected in an artistic production is granted to designers. The main point I wanted to get across to the art crowd audience is that graphic design is also a vehicle for personal expression and conviction, not just a slick commercially complicit service. It was important that the design did not reflect a bias towards any one particular aesthetic or ideology. In a situation like this the strategy often used is to design a clean, modern, neutral format. I rejected this approach because there is nothing "neutral" about modernism and nothing particularly "clean" about the avant garde. I did not approach the calendars as a "problem" to be solved but as an opportunity to be explored. I used several of my own typefaces before they were fine tuned, as well as software applications I barely understood. There are many details in these pieces that are not refined and some things I tried did not come out as I would have liked, but that is the nature of experimentation. Designers often extol the virtues of "experimental work" and "risk taking" but only within the safe parameters of what is deemed "appropriate" and "professional". This amounts to nothing more than "novelty" – taking what is already accepted and doing something slightly different with it. Without the possibility of failure there is no experimentation. Too often graphic designers tend to equate all failure with a lack of professionalism rather than considering it a necessary step in advancing design.

DESIGNER

Mr. Keedy

CLIENT

Los Angeles Contemporary Exhibitions

TYPOGRAPHER

Mr. Keedy

PRINTER

Glendale Rotery Press

PAPER

Newspaper

OBJECTIVES

Generate inquiry, inform and educate, introduce

AUDIENCE

Art community

RV

What I like about the LACE Calendars is their weird typography on the front: information through entertainment. It's very well organized, as is the actual calendar on the other side: information through organization. There's a recognizable consistency to this concept, which shows that one designer is responsible for the series.

Madonna: The Immaculate Collection
RETAIL CD DIGIPAK

ENTRANT'S COMMENTS

The inspiration for this package came in part from Madonna's "Blonde Ambition" tour, and in part from the Herb Ritts photo session used inside the package. In the photos, Madonna appears as though part of a twisted theater carnival – part clown, part burlesque queen. In the live show, she prances in outrageous Gaultier-designed outfits: corsets, knee pads, papal robes, polka dots. The logo design started as a reference to the corset shape, complete with dangling tassels. Satin was chosen for its preciousness. Typographically, we tried to tap into the pious aspects of Madonna's personna by adopting a rigid style. Blood red, french blue, metallic gold, and an unexpected green were consciously chosen to enhance the confusion. Is this serious or is this silly? Is this beautiful or in poor taste?

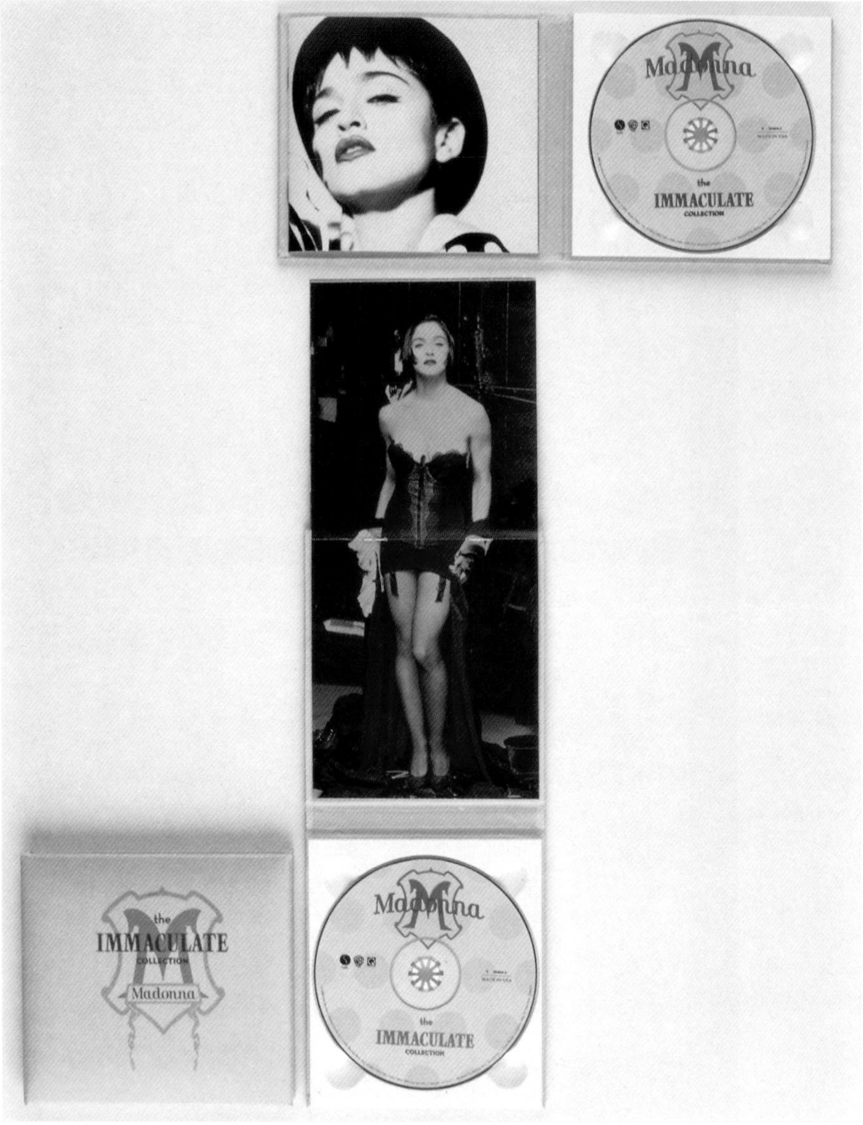

DESIGNERS
Jeri Heiden, John Heiden

ART DIRECTOR
Jeri Heiden

WRITER
Gene Sculatti

PHOTOGRAPHER
Herb Ritts

DESIGN FIRM
Warner Bros. Records

CLIENT
Sire Records

TYPOGRAPHER
Aldus Type Studio

OBJECTIVE
Generate interest in recording artist

AUDIENCES
Radio and retail

RV

This is Madonna! This is what she is to a lot of her fans. In Europe, Madonna's recent film "Truth or Dare" is called "In Bed With Madonna." That's what this CD package is: In Bed With Madonna.

ENTRANT'S COMMENTS

The Issaac Mizrahi ads were made to reverse the coldness and "attitude" of most high fashion advertising. The viewer is brought into the process of making fashion. Nick Waplington's photography is documentary. It reveals the pressure, ad-hocism, collaboration and thinking that goes into creating a collection.

DESIGNERS

Tibor Kalman, Emily Oberman

PHOTOGRAPHER

Nick Waplington

DESIGN FIRM

M&Co.

CLIENT

Isaac Mizrahi

TYPOGRAPHER

M&Co.

OBJECTIVES

Generate inquiry, support of sales, document

AUDIENCE

Consumer

ISAAC MIZRAHI
Bergdorf Goodman

RV

Great art direction. I love Nick Waplington's photography and his would be snap-shot quality. It has more to it than meets the eye. I appreciate the fact that the photograph is respected; it doesn't bleed off the page and isn't destroyed by the typography. A wonderful ad.

ENTRANT'S COMMENTS

The design of these fonts came out of my desire to move beyond the traditional concerns of type designers, such as elegance and legibility; to produce typographic forms which bring to language additional levels of meaning; and to trade in this myth of the transparency of typographic form for a more realistic attitude toward form, acknowledging that form carries meaning. These faces are based on the realization that Helvetica is ultimately idiosyncratic, because that kind of supreme reductiveness requires a pathological commitment to consistency which is rare, even among designers. Form is functional, because everything is read. Template Gothic and Template Gothic Bold combine references to vernacular design (the lettering template) with references to professional modes of design production (tapered letterforms, truncated strokes, letters that look like bad photomechanical reproductions) and a whimsical treatment of symbols within type (ampersAND, etc.). Industry San Serif combines references to many of my favorite sans serif faces (Metro, Gill, Bell Gothic) with some serifs (a welcome addition to any sans serif alphabet). The intent was to create my own Helvetica: just as idiosyncratic, but without the pretensions. A bouncy baseline and truncated numerals contribute to the personality of this face.

Template Gothic Bold

ABCDEFGHIJKLMN
OPQRSTUVWXYZ
abcdefghijklmnop
qrstuvwxyz
[1234567890]
№‒at!%$ampers-AND&?

Industry Sans Serif

ABCDEFGHIJKLMN
OPQRSTUVWXYZ
abcdefghijklmnop
qrstuvwxyz
[1234567890]
№@!%$&?

DESIGNER
Barry Deck

WRITER
Rudy Vanderlans/Emigre

PHOTOGRAPHER
Barry Deck

DESIGN FIRM
Barry Deck Design

PUBLISHER
Emigre

PRINTER
LaserWriter IINT

RV

This imperfect type reflects more truly the imperfect nature of an imperfect world, inhabited by imperfect human beings. Some details I find very attractive. There are also a couple of funny, daring things, like cutting off the top of the number one. Now and then it looks almost out of focus, but it works. It's a very usable and legible type, even in small point sizes. And what interests me the most is that it's computer generated but doesn't look like it.

ENTRANT'S COMMENTS

The objective of the Nynex annual report was to communicate their efforts in confronting the four primary forces driving the communications industry. To illustrate these forces, we used an editorial style, summarized by a word, a sentence and a paragraph. The report's design needed to be friendly (to affect people, especially employees), distinctive (from other Bell companies), informative (easy to read), and innovative (to show leadership).

DESIGNER

David Suh

ART DIRECTORS

Kent Hunter, Aubrey Balkind

WRITER

Sean Healey

ILLUSTRATOR

James Yang

PHOTOGRAPHER

Michael Melford

DESIGN FIRM

Frankfurt Gips Balkind

CLIENT

NYNEX Corporation

OBJECTIVES

Generate inquiry, inform and educate, support of sales

AUDIENCES

Corporate, internal, consumer

American Center for Design FOURTEENTH ANNUAL **100** SHOW

RV

This was a relief: one of the only annual reports I saw that stood out. The combination of images and typewriter typography works very well. Giving it a magazine quality is a great idea, one which makes it easier to find information. It communicates better than the usual annual report, with its essay and numbers in the back.

Pen Plus STATIONERY

ENTRANT'S COMMENTS

The client is a communication consulting firm in Japan. The juxtaposition of the contemporary (color) and traditional (printing) reflects the client's business philosophy.

DESIGNER
Takaaki Matsumoto
ART DIRECTORS
Takaaki Matsumoto, Michael McGinn
DESIGN FIRM
M Plus M Incorporated
CLIENT
Pen Plus Inc.
TYPOGRAPHER
M Plus M Incorporated
PRINTER
Continental-Bournique Ltd.

RV

The typography is quite straight-forward, but through the use of day-glo inks and simple embossing a special quality is added. It's very attractive and well executed.

Performance POSTCARDS

It was suggested by the art diector, Caryn Aono, to use an inexpensive florescent stock and to follow the format from the previous year: creating one piece of art to print in two colors on three separate colors of stock. This was done to keep costs low andto distinguish an identity for each school represented within the series. The paper stock created the illusion of a third ink color, further distinguishing each school. For the design of the series as a whole, I attempted a performance on FreeHand by using the basic tools, making shapes, grouping, enlarging, and turning images on the screen that were no longer there once the mouse was released; ephemeral images seen on the monitor but that are impossible to save or laserprint. This image inspired me to recapture it and to specify on tissue to the printer to manipulate it even further during the offset printing process. Caryn and I expected color shifts to occur each time the inks would absorb into the different colors of stock, but not even the printer could be certain exactly what colors would finally be acheived. This made the printing process a sort of Russian roulette: it was hit or miss. I guess we were lucky.

DESIGNER

Robin Cottle

ART DIRECTOR

Caryn Aono

DESIGN FIRM

CalArts Public Affairs Office

CLIENT

CalArts

PRINTER

Stacey Hauge Printing

OBJECTIVES

Inform and educate, introduce

AUDIENCE

Consumer

American Center for Design FOURTEENTH ANNUAL **100** SHOW

RV

These six cards have a neo-psychedelic quality to them, probably because of the choice of colors and the use of free form shapes which develop into their own language over different events. The work from CalArts seems rooted in a populism, in pop culture. Maybe it's the west coast and rock and roll. Yeah.

Admissions Portfolio Days POSTER

ENTRANT'S COMMENTS

I was asked to make an "eye-catching" poster without making the poster look too text heavy, even though the copy provided was six pages long. I had a tight deadline, and before having time to panic I sat at the computer and started simultaneously typing and designing, rearranging and restructuring, connecting text from one page with information from another. I felt as if I was a composer playing the keyboard at a piano. A process of modulation started taking place; using the manipulable, liquid-like capabilities of FreeHand allowed me to move the information throughout the space. After the design was complete, I realized that my approach was an intuitive response to the text provided. It made sense to rearrange the text so that the reader could receive various modes of information when needed.

DESIGNER

Robin Cottle

DESIGN FIRM

CalArts Public Affairs Office

CLIENT

CalArts

PRINTER

ProLitho

PAPER

Curtis Tuscan Terra

OBJECTIVES

Inform and educate

AUDIENCES

Prospective students and their parents

RV

I've got this on my wall at home. I like it a lot. This is a poster which acts as both a poster and brochure. We in Europe are not familiar with the phenomenon of an indoor poster, probably because of our culture of walking. This has great clarity and provides a lot of information on different levels through an intelligently designed hierarchy of type and color.

CalArts Postcards

We took the idea of the "Greetings From…" postcards (but not the style) to make these inquiry cards. The typography on the back was deliberately designed to look un-designed or generic. By using as little "style" as possible, the focus is on the "idea" of a location and the activity that takes place within it. The student simply detaches the reply card at the bottom to send for admission information. The remaining postcards can be detached and sent to friends.

DESIGNERS

Edward Fella, Jeffery Keedy,
Lorraine Wild, P. Lyn Middleton

ILLUSTRATOR

Edward Fella

PHOTOGRAPHER

Edward Fella

CLIENT

CalArts

PRINTER

Donahue Printing, LA

OBJECTIVES

Inform and educate, introduce

AUDIENCES

Recruitment of students and their
parents

American Center for Design FOURTEENTH ANNUAL **100** SHOW

RV

These postcards look like random snapshots taken almost anywhere in the US. Most people don't send postcards that only show the top of a building and part of a tree. The type layer functions as a keyhole through which the different disciplines are projected. It tells you more about their purpose and makes the receiver think. Great, simple ideas make people think. It would be fun to receive these in the post.

Relax MAGAZINE COVER

ENTRANT'S COMMENTS

I was asked to design a cover for the short-lived magazine So. The publication's glossy stock, "expensive" look, and free monthly distribution was part of an overall endeavor to promote recreational activities and to support local advertisers' messages and other various propaganda. Inspiration came from a three hour long experiment which involved sitting in front of a television armed only with a remote control. Baudrillard viewed advertising as an invasion of public and private space which is reduced to a "large soft body with many heads." In this publication, as in television, content is replaced with advertising, language becomes hype. The suggestion to "relax" is subverted by the image of the surrounding text, thus implying that one should be anything but relaxed in their media-generated environment.

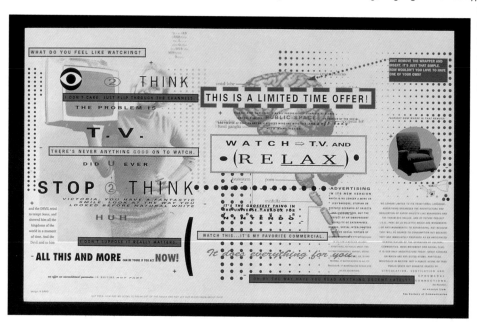

DESIGNER

Robert Sirko

DESIGN FIRM

R Sirko Design

CLIENT

So Magazine

TYPOGRAPHER

Robert Sirko

PRINTER

Home Moutain Press

SEPARATOR

Advertiser's Aid

PAPER

Productolith Gloss

OBJECTIVE

Promote

RV

Watch TV and relax – that's what you shouldn't do. One should go out, see and discover things. That's what this piece tells you. At first I thought it was a poster, and I'm usually not fond of too much layering on a poster; it disguises the message. When I discovered it was a magazine, it became an intriguing piece. Sit down, relax, read this magazine, go out and experience the world. This piece has to do with message through entertainment.

90

REM: Out of Time
LIMITED EDITION PORTFOLIO CD PACKAGE

ENTRANT'S COMMENTS

This project uses a wide range of images; thus it needed a system that allowed each contribution a chance to be viewed on its own terms, while retaining an overall sense of unification. The loose-leaf format of a postcard portfolio created such a format. The actual construction of the portfolio was an attempt to present these images in a natural way that involved the viewer. Each set of postcards was printed on five different recycled stocks that rotated in a sequence of somewhat unique, albeit subtle, groupings.

DESIGNERS

Tom Recchion, Michael Stipe

DESIGN FIRM

Warner Bros. Records

CLIENT

Warner Bros. Records

PRINTER

Westland Graphics

SEPARATOR

Color Service

PAPERS

Evergreen, Sihl Vellum, Fasson
Pastel Offset

OBJECTIVE

Generate interest in recording artist

AUDIENCES

Radio and retail

RV

To be honest, I'm not too keen on the whole package, with all the postcards by different artists. Who needs them? But when you get through all these extras you find a precious little gem: a vellum dustcover with a wooden CD inside. To change the appearance of the material is a great and simple idea. The plastic becomes wood. It almost becomes an object in and of itself.

Sex Goddess POSTER

ENTRANT'S COMMENTS

The photographs for this critical piece about fashion for a little magazine called Revenge were first taken on a hotel balcony looking over Sunset Boulevard. They never worked out for the magazine because as far as I know there was never a second issue. We then reconstructed the photos digitally and with language in response to an invitation by ID Magazine for their fantasy portfolio to "Redesign a California Stereotype". The piece was rejected for "gratuitous nudity". Unfortunately, the editors may have missed the point entirely, which, for us, contributes to the liberation of sexual stereotypes and Hollywood mythology, particularly its fetishization of nudity.

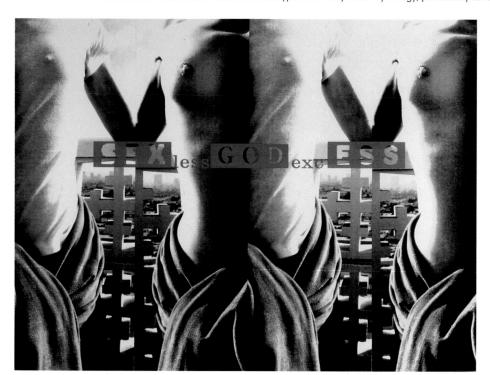

DESIGNERS
P. Scott Makela,
Laurie Haycock Makela
PHOTOGRAPHER
P. Scott Makela
PRINTER
Linotronic/Silkscreen
OBJECTIVE
Stimulate

RV

This is a powerful personal piece, and is clear and direct. The images tell what text says. I like the different reading levels and the cheapness of the production.

Sex Goddess POSTER

Terrell: On The Wings of Dirty Angels
PROMOTIONAL CD DIGIPAK

ENTRANT'S COMMENTS

I designed the outer portion of this package with the idea that it might age well over time and take on the quality of a beautifully made book; old books have a mysterious and knowing quality all their own. I tried to reflect the band's gritty, sensual, Bible Belt rock in my choice of photography. The concept of a "Dirty Angel" came from the band and symbolizes the group members' Southern and sordid roots.

DESIGNER

Kim Champagne

PHOTOGRAPHER

Mark Abrahams

DESIGN FIRM

Warner Bros. Records

CLIENT

Giant Records

TYPOGRAPHER

Aldus Type Studio

PRINTER

AGI

SEPARATOR

Color Service

PAPER

Gloss book

OBJECTIVE

Generate interest in recording artist

AUDIENCES

Radio and retail

RV

If there's one design I really dislike it's plastic CD boxes. They often break and you can never get the booklet out without completely ripping it to pieces. This type of CD package gives the designer the opportunity to design. This is very attractive packaging, with good typography, nicely chosen materials and a lovely booklet.

Tripper LOGO

ENTRANT'S COMMENTS

Tripper is a dog safety harness for your car, designed for travel safety. The logo had to be simple enough to be stitched onto a label, and needed to convey a sense of the "happy auto-bound hound."

DESIGNER
Robert Sirko

ART DIRECTOR
Robert Sirko

DESIGN FIRM
R Sirko Design

CLIENT
The Christopher Corporation

RV

This logo tells you what it's for, which is quite an accomplishment nowadays. I hate logos that don't tell you anything, that are just a blob and don't give you any information about the company or the product. This logo works.

Yo Booklet

ENTRANT'S COMMENTS

Having worked independently as a designer/illustrator since 1977 in the US and Europe, I founded my own design studio, Rosenworld, Inc., in 1989. Everybody claims to be diverse and multidisciplinary but we're not kidding around. Some people find this confusing. We want to help these people out but we refuse to limit ourselves. This adaptable brochure gives us a way to address each kind of client with projects that clearly relate to their particular needs. Client-specific, interchangeable pages show through a die-cut cover, which outlines our company's capabilities in brilliant, witty prose.

DESIGNER

Laurie Rosenwald

WRITER

Laurie Rosenwald

DESIGN FIRM

Rosenworld, Inc.

CLIENT

Rosenworld, Inc.

TYPOGRAPHER

CT Photogenics

PRINTER

Terwilliger, Inc.

SEPARATOR

Terwilliger, Inc.

PAPER

Simpson

OBJECTIVES

Generate inquiry, inform and educate

AUDIENCE

Corporate

RV

The design of this piece seems to reflect her work quite well. I like the idea of inserting different pages within the same cover for different clients. Colorful communication is what it says and what it is.

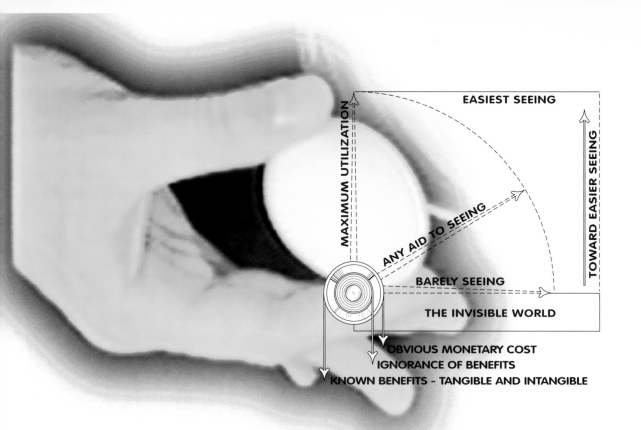

MAXIMUM UTILIZATION

EASIEST SEEING

ANY AID TO SEEING

TOWARD EASIER SEEING

BARELY SEEING

THE INVISIBLE WORLD

OBVIOUS MONETARY COST
IGNORANCE OF BENEFITS
KNOWN BENEFITS - TANGIBLE AND INTANGIBLE

BRUCE **Mau** SELECTIONS

Above the Law BROCHURE

This piece was developed for a national union organization. The intent of the brochure was to present a hard-hitting picture of certain non-union, Las Vegas casinos that were known to be breaking the law; abusing employees; kidnapping, beating and robbing customers; and managed by certain "families" with questionable moral values and work ethics. The brochure needed to communicate immediate, strong visual messages to its audience. It was intended to shock the reader with its brutal use of photography and disturbing color and background patterns. The concept was a real challenge to execute, especially given the fact that we were required to use images and photographs provided to us by the client, and assemble them in a way that would best relay the urgency of the situation.

DESIGNER

Lois Nightingale

ART DIRECTOR

Paula Jaworski

DESIGN FIRM

J. Gibson & Company

CLIENT

Culinary Workers Union, Local 226

TYPOGRAPHER

Wordscape

PRINTER

Affilated Graphics

SEPARATOR

Art & Negative Graphics

PAPER

Warrenflo

OBJECTIVES

Generate inquiry, inform and educate

AUDIENCES

Corporate, consumer

American Center for Design FOURTEENTH ANNUAL 100 SHOW

BM

This is a very strange agglomeration. They are using a very serious set of accusations to get support for the union, and have designed a rather slick piece that could be distributed in a news magazine. It is where the style hits the content that an interesting fissure is created.

Adobe Caslon BOOKLET

The design of a type specimen book strives to be an ideal context for the presentation of a typeface family. Everything – the text, the artwork, the sequencing – contributes to letting the types do the work they were designed for.

DESIGNER

Laurie Szujewska

EDITOR

Tanya Wendling

DESIGN FIRM

Adobe Systems Inc.

CLIENT

Adobe Systems Inc.

TYPOGRAPHERS

Laurie Szjewska, James Young, Ewa Gaurielow

PRINTER

West Coast Litho

PAPER

Mohawk Superfine

OBJECTIVES

Inform and educate, introduce

AUDIENCE

Consumer

BM

Beautiful, elegant and refined.

Air Canada 1990 ANNUAL REPORT

The 1990 Air Canada Annual Report reflects a "low key" yet sophisticated approach using black and white photography, a classical layout and recycled paper. The panoramic and theatrical views emphasize superior service and employee dedication.

DESIGNER
Sylvain Allard

ART DIRECTOR
Peter Steiner

WRITERS
Denis Chagnon, Denis Biro

PHOTOGRAPHER
Bernard Bohn

DESIGN FIRM
Gottschalk+Ash International

CLIENT
Air Canada

TYPOGRAPHER
Centre Typographique

PRINTER
Mathews, Ingham & Lake

SEPARATOR
Ind. Tri-Graphiques

PAPER
Retreeve

OBJECTIVE
Document

AUDIENCES
Corporate, shareholder

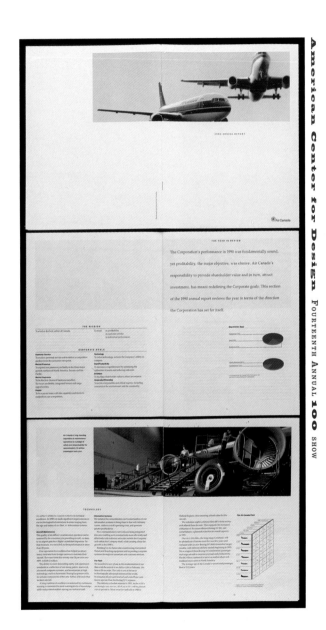

American Center for Design FOURTEENTH ANNUAL **100** SHOW

BM

This has the quality of people carrying out their own project, and an honest tone. A friend of mine once sent me a tape in which he was talking about art, and he said "Art is something you can trust, and there is not a lot of art floating around these days." There is something about this piece that makes me want to trust it.

Blueprints for Learning:

The "Blueprints for Learning" posters were designed as part of a research and design project for Apple Computer, Inc., in conjunction with Apple Classrooms of Tommorrow (ACOT). The goal of the project was two-fold: first, to identify emerging trends in theories of learning, and second, to communicate these trends so that they could support the design of new technologies to enhance learning. The conceptual framework we created from the research consisted of six basic themes that describe qualities found in positive learning environments. The posters were one of several forms through which we communicated the findings of our research. The poster also had

a special use as part of a design workshop at the annual ACOT Open House, in which their role was to convey the content of the themes quickly to a varied audience consisting of students, teachers, researchers and designers. In addition to allowing us to create more effective forms of communication, our approach gave us a way to embody the themes themselves, resulting in artifacts that are examples of how the themes can be used in design.

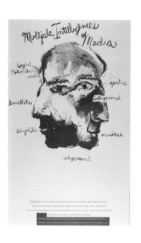

DESIGNERS
Christopher Pacione, Tim Best, Kate Welker

PROGRAM MANAGER
John Rheinfrank

WRITERS
Kate Welker, Tim Best

ILUSTRATOR
Christopher Pacione

DESIGN FIRM
Fitch RichardsonSmith

CLIENT
Apple Computer, Inc.

TYPOGRAPHER
Harlan Type

PRINTER
West Camp Press

OBJECTIVES
Inform and educate

AUDIENCES
Internal, consumer

BM

This is a very quiet and modest series of works that addresses serious content. The way these are edited, organized and written is very, very good, and the images are beautiful. Each has been printed in just one color. A lot of other people would not have handled these so modestly.

ENTRANT'S COMMENTS

This annual report, a year-end review of a multi-disciplinary art school, is written in a clear and straightforward manner. The design reflects this through the handled modestly typography on a generous page accompanied by small black and white portraits of the people and places that comprise the Institute.

DESIGNER

Caryn Aono

WRITER

Diane Saltzberg

DESIGN FIRM

CalArts Office of Public Affairs

CLIENT

CalArts

PAPER

Hopper Cardigan, Quintessence Gloss

OBJECTIVES

Inform and educate

AUDIENCES

Corporate, internal

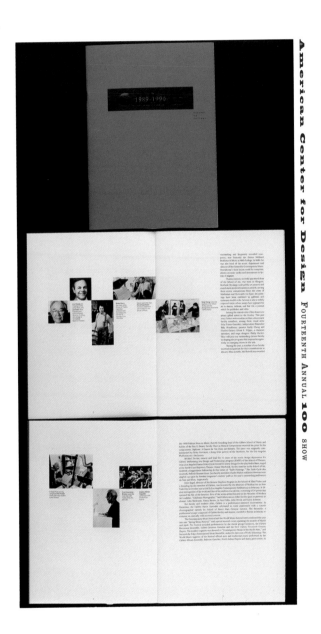

American Center for Design FOURTEENTH ANNUAL 100 SHOW

BM

A very quiet typographic environment allows the reader to enter the text quite easily, as does the simple treatment of the images. A straightforward and refreshing piece of work.

CalArts STATIONERY

ENTRANT'S COMMENTS

The interesting aspect of this project was creating a color palette large enough to distinguish the nine divisions within the Institute. This required color combinations that were distinct, yet did not create a rainbow spectrum when viewed together. The final color choices were influenced by the Duo Color Guide, a 1948 reference book on duotones. The unexpected color combinations of the CalArts stationery came from studying these older color demonstrations. An ordering device to distinguish between the administration and the schools was also acheived through color. The schools share a common black and the administration and its divisions are limited to a specific green and blue and the combinations of these cool colors.

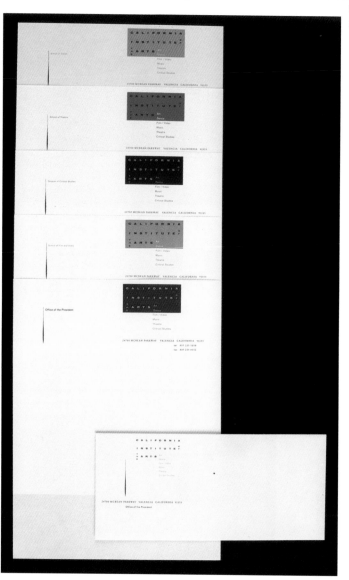

DESIGNER
Lisa Nugent

DESIGN FIRM
CalArts Public Affairs Office

CLIENT
CalArts

PRINTER
Donahue Printing

PAPER
Strathmore

OBJECTIVES
Generate inquiry, inform and educate

AUDIENCE
Internal

BM

This is an exceptional piece of typography. The way the colors work and the way the system works is not really earth shattering; it's the detail work that really separates this piece from the others. The individual color combinations and the very subtle relationships from one piece of text to another have been smartly resolved. It seems like very time consuming and meticulous work.

Designer Series Speaker System BROCHURE

ENTRANT'S COMMENTS

This brochure was conceived to be a high-end data sheet with the functionality of a brochure. Conceptually, the piece needed to convey the attributes of the product, the most important being that the speakers offer excellent sound quality with a minimum amount of obtrusiveness (the speakers are relatively small in size and mount flush with the wall when installed). By making the piece the actual size of the largest speaker in the series and having a perforated cover, the prospective buyer can visualize the product in their home as realistically as possible.

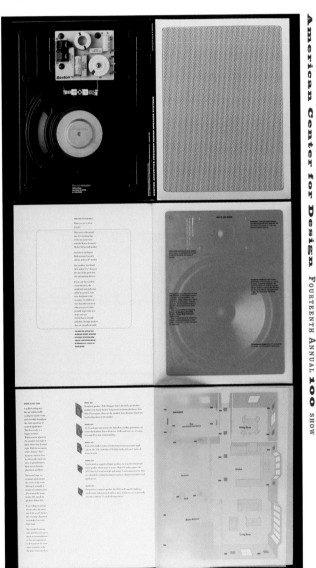

(right margin, vertical text) American Center for Design FOURTEENTH ANNUAL 100 SHOW

DESIGNERS

Bruce Crocker, Martin Sorger

ART DIRECTOR

Bruce Crocker

WRITER

Ray Welch

PHOTOGRAPHER

John Shotwell

DESIGN FIRM

Crocker Inc.

CLIENT

Boston

TYPOGRAPHER

Williams Typography

PRINTER

Nimrod Press

PAPER

Celesta Gloss, UV UltraII

OBJECTIVES

Generate inquiry, inform and educate, introduce, support of sales

AUDIENCE

Consumer

BM

This piece takes the product, which seems exceptionally well designed, and uses it as the basis for its own format. It's cleanly put together, intelligently formatted, good communication. It's rare when the designer of product communication materials actually understands the qualities of the product and brings them to the fore. More often, you don't get a sense of what those qualities are; you get a pitch to lifestyle. This is not a pitch to lifestyle; this is a pitch to design. This is a quality product. I want to get these right away.

Ecodea PROMOTIONAL BROCHURE

The booklet is an introduction to Ecodea, an environmental consultancy serving the advertising, packaging and publishing industries. The Ecodea concept provides practical environmental strategies for imaging and marketing projects. The consultancy is based on the theory that sound environmental decisions do not end with good engineering, such as recycled and recyclable materials, but must also include good and timeless ideas. The booklets were published with the following objectives: to launch the division, to tell a short story of the need for such perspective with design, and to demonstrate of what sensitive engineering joined with a sensitive idea can produce. The Ecodea booklet was letterpressed using handset metal type, the most basic form of recycled typography. The stock is entirely reclaimed kraft paperboard. Colored inks are water-based and hand applied. The booklet was bound without glues and is held with an easily-removed screw set. The piece doubles as a business card for each of the four partners in the consultancy.

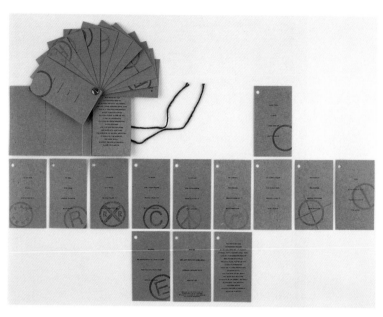

DESIGNERS

Debi Young Mees, Diane Gilleland

ART DIRECTORS

Forrest Richardson, Valerie Richardson

WRITER

Forrest Richardson

DESIGN FIRM

Richardson or Richardson

CLIENT

Ecodea

TYPOGRAPHER

McGrew Printing

PRINTER

McGrew Printing

PAPER

Recycled chipboard

OBJECTIVES

Generate inquiry, inform and educate, introduce

AUDIENCE

Corporate

BM

This is actually a fairly responsible way of dealing with promoting an ecologically sound practice. The piece is almost entirely idea, with very little additional stuff. In a way, it addresses the real problem. Somehow we have to come into a sustainable ecology, but at the same time there must be an allowance for excess, because it's in the way that a culture manipulates its excess and directs its success that is the mark of the culture. This little piece actually gets down to the fact that people do business and that we must figure out a way of conducting that trade in the most economical and ecologically sound way.

Framework Vol. 4 Magazine

Hopefully the visual (physical) lie of the cover was as thought provoking as it was annoying to deal with. The physical misinformation was obviously intentional to help reinforce the content of the articles and concept of the issue. It would have been nice to have scented it with Obsession.

DESIGNER

Michael Fink

DESIGN FIRM

x height

CLIENT

Los Angeles Center for
Photographic Studies

TYPOGRAPHER

x height

PRINTER

Navigator Press

SEPARATOR

Navigator

OBJECTIVES

Inform and educate, document

AUDIENCES

Consumer, art patrons

American Center for Design FOURTEENTH ANNUAL **100** SHOW

BM

This is a very funny idea, the idea of an issue on misinformation with a cover that's upside down. When you open the cover and see the last page of the ads you realize that you've been duped. The inside of the book is quite nice.

Holiday Card

Every argument has two sides; each side has its adherents. For each person who detests Arafat, there is a person who detests Shamir. With the threat of war coming in the Middle East last December, we felt it was important to point out – in a light manner – the self-evident but difficult proposition that peace is possible only when people embrace it, that peace is a larger issue than taking sides. So we tried to compile a rogue's gallery of world leaders, mindful of Mikhail Gorbachev's treatment of the Baltic republics, Erich Honneker's murderous policies in East Germany, Francois Mitterand's sabotage of Greenpeace's anti-nuclear efforts in the South Pacific, George Bush's invasion of Panama, Yasser Arafat's attacks against Israel, and Deng Xiaoping's massacre of the pro-democracy students in Tien An Min Square. Each of these men, in the name of some higher goal, has blood on his hands.

Each of these men controls people and weapons capable of wreaking havoc upon his fellow men, and it is in the hands of these men (among others) that any realization of peace rests. The card became a reminder of the unlikely condition of peace in this world. And besides, it's funny.

DESIGNER
David Horton

ART DIRECTOR
John Kane

WRITER
John Kane

DESIGN FIRM
Sametz Blackstone Associates

CLIENT
Sametz Blackstone Associates

TYPOGRAPHER
Graphics Express

PRINTER
Reynolds-DeWalt

OBJECTIVES
Generate inquiry

BM

Its simplicity and clarity are appropriate for its message.

Inquiries: Language in Art

I am exploring the relationship between the content of design decisions and the representation of works of art. What is an appropriate relationship? What relationships are possible? This catalog attempts one response. The work in "Inquiries: Language in Art" sustains a debased material aspect; the artists favor process over conventional aesthetic concerns. I responded to this by adopting a parallel strategy. I chose to make the articulation of the various components of the book evident, not to embellish them, with the exception of the cover. Gerald Ferguson allowed his "Length 4" from "The Standard Corpus of Present Day English Usage", arranged by word length, to be wrapped around the book, letterpressed into cardboard in pink ink. "Length 4" is used as generic information rather than as a reproduction of a work of art. The reciprocity between "Length 4" and its capacity to illustrate the book's contents is consistent with the spirit of the exhibition in general and this work in particular.

DESIGNER

Lisa Naftolin

WRITER

Christina Ritchie

DESIGN FIRM

Art Gallery of Ontario

CLIENT

Art Gallery of Ontario

TYPOGRAPHER

The TypeCrafters Inc.

PRINTERS

Provincial Graphics Inc., Lunar
Caustic Press

SEPARATOR

Herzig Somerville Ltd.

PAPER

Lustro Dull, Domtar Bond

OBJECTIVES

Inform and educate, document

AUDIENCE

People who are interested in
contemporary art

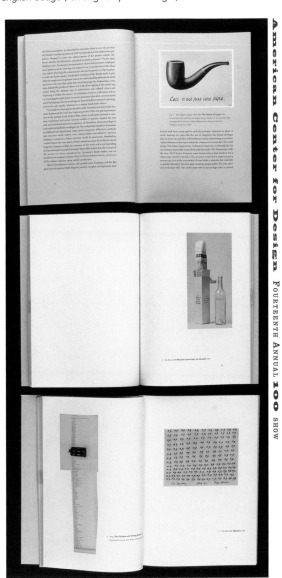

BM

This is a good idea for an exhibition and the catalog reflects that. It has the classic qualities that are good in a catalog: a modest intervention by the designer, a clear representation of the works, a certain meticulousness to the way the things are ordered on the pages, and a nice rhythm to the way the pages are designed. Typographically, it's very well resolved.

The Kill-Off POSTER

ENTRANT'S COMMENTS

More than the plot, it was the deep, dark mood of this film, adapted from the equally dark Jim Thompson novel, that we wanted to evoke. Although the film had an excellent ensemble cast, there were no recognizable stars that we were compelled to feature. Using this to advantage, we kept people out of the design to convey the desolation one experiences watching the film. The plot, which revolves around a wicked invalid who manipulates the town's inhabitants through telephone gossip, was reduced to its essence: the power of her words.

DESIGNERS
Jennifer Schumacher, Jennifer Washburn

ART DIRECTOR
Thomas Starr

WRITER
Thomas Starr

DESIGN FIRM
Thomas Starr & Associates

CLIENT
Cabriolet Films

TYPOGRAPHERS
The Typecrafters, Black Ink Typographers

PRINTER
Continental Litho

SEPARATOR
Continental Litho

OBJECTIVE
Introduce

AUDIENCE
Consumer

BM

I think that they have managed to turn a restriction to their advantage and make quite a rarity: a film poster that is beautiful. There aren't too many of those around these days.

Lovecamp 7: The Green Album

ENTRANT'S COMMENTS

The problem: Create an all type, three color cover for a young band that fused psychedelic sounds with an ironic sense of humor and clever lyrics, especially one that left me with a lasting image: "Janice in a green light, like she's standing over a xerox machine…" The solution: Use type and layout to suggest the 1960s and get that green light in there with a sense of humor. I used the dark background colors to make the bright script pop electrically and to repeat the band's name (they needed the publicity and I needed an image of some sort) while remaining somewhat subtle.

DESIGNER

Jessica Shatan

DESIGN FIRM

The Sarabande Press

CLIENT

Lovecamp 7

PUBLISHER

Barkley & Surrey

TYPOGRAPHER

Kennedy Typographers

PRINTER

RHM Industries

PAPER

James River

OBJECTIVES

Generate inquiry, package and protect, support of sales

AUDIENCE

Consumer

BM

Their stated objective was to design an all type album cover that would convey the offbeat, quirky style of the band and evoke their influences from the 1950s and 1960s. Absolutely successful, I would say. It recalls those ideas and stylistic conventions, yet maintains a currency.

Mead Moistrite Matte PROMOTION

ENTRANT'S COMMENTS

I was hired by Mead to design a promotional piece for Moistrite Matte that would vie for attention amidst the glut of paper samples that cross the desks of designers, advertisers and printers. The primary function of the piece was to show the printability of the paper. Since Moistrite is a matte paper, great care was taken to design with the paper's limitations in mind. Care was also taken to try to entertain the viewer. The word "matte" seemed to be key. Puns using the word "mat," as in "doormat," were engineered from cover to cover to playfully interpret with photographs and illustrations such mats as "maternity," "matador," "matural history," and others. The hope was to leave no doubt after 20 pages that one had received an entertaining book printed well on Moistrite Matte.

DESIGNER
Bryan L. Peterson

WRITER
Margaret Watson

PHOTOGRAPHER
Tom Ryan

DESIGN FIRM
Peterson & Company

CLIENT
Mead Fine Paper Division

TYPOGRAPHER
Creative type

PRINTER
Padgett Printing

PAPER
Mead Moistrite Matte

OBJECTIVES
Generate inquiry, inform and educate, introduce

AUDIENCES
Corporate, internal, consumer

BM

This image is just great.

Mind Over Matter CATALOG

ENTRANT'S COMMENTS

The exhibition program of the Whitney Museum is known for introducing new art work and art movements. The exhibition "Mind Over Matter" presented the work of six sculptors who deal with highly emotional and politically charged issues in a cool, pseudo-scientific manner. The exhibition catalog was designed to present this intentionally disturbing dichotomy between the intense subject matter and the dispassionate presentation. The logical, classical format and sequence of the book alludes to the rational, systematic quality of the art. The catalog's unconventional typography, cover stock and ink color, the small-scaled invitation, and the M/M symbol developed to signify the show combined to express the unsettling effect of this art.

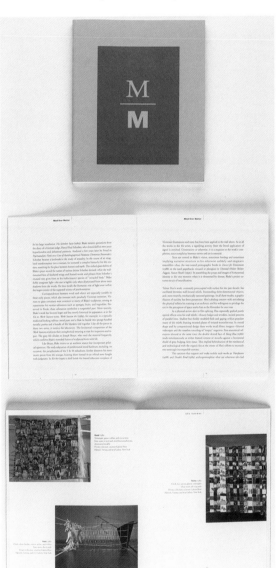

DESIGNER

Anita Meyer

CURATOR

Richard Armstrong

HEAD OF PUBLICATIONS

Doris Palca

DESIGN FIRM

plus design inc.

CLIENT

Whitney Museum of American Art

TYPOGRAPHER

Monotype Composition Company

PRINTER

Meridian Printing

PAPERS

Champion Cordwain, Champion Pageantry, Curtis Tuscan Terra

OBJECTIVES

Inform and educate, document

AUDIENCES

All

BM

For the most part this does what I would ask of such a project. It presents the material clearly, it's well produced, it's easy to move through the book, and for the most part it's easy to read. The pages, however, are all capitals, which I think is generally a mistake in a book. The interview sections, where there are blocks of text set in bold sans serif type interspersed with serif type, I don't think are very effective. But on a whole I think it is a very effective book. Beautifully done.

ENTRANT'S COMMENTS

The concept for output was proposed by my third year visual communication students at Herron School of Art to the Herron Chapter of Students in Design. The students wanted to explore the idea of establishing a dialog among design and art students throughout the country. It was our intent that this piece would act as a springboard for others to answer our thoughts and to research their own concerns. The topic for the first edition of output was order and chaos, a scientific principle that was used as a metaphor for our sociological concerns. In reviewing the process of creating output, perhaps the students said it best: "This periodical is an attempt to tap into a realm of influence beyond the classroom and to establish a communicative network. We, the producers of this edition, are students. We feel that this status, along with our geographical location, isolates us. The periodical output can be anything, any format or medium, as long as a dialog is established, as long as something is said."

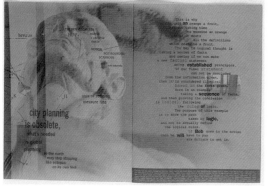

DESIGNERS

Rob Bonds, Fred Bower, Klynn Dunkin, Jim Ozolilis

ART DIRECTOR

Joani Spadaro

WRITERS

Mike Trice, Mark Davis

ARTISTS

Mike Hall, Pam Halliburton, Rich Barker, Scott Ramone, Angie Richardson

DESIGN FIRM

Herron School of Art Chapter, Students in Design

PRINTER

White Arts

PAPER

ESSE

OBJECTIVES

Generate inquiry, inform and educate

AUDIENCES

Students, design schools, universities, visual artists and design professionals

BM

This is quite an interesting experiment. The design of the material is well integrated with the content. It has some interesting ideas in it: that order and chaos are two forms of order, for example. The interesting thing is the designer moving towards content. They are using the technology available to actually engage material of their own, which is a new way for designers to work, especially design students. In a lot of schools you see dummy copy instead of real words. In this case you actually have engaging information and engaging content and students trying to deal with the problem of being an editor and a designer.

Printing Clean CATALOG

ENTRANT'S COMMENTS

Printing clean means designing clean. Earth. Air. Water. Elemental units. Elemental design. Use the air of paper, the breadth of pure space, the naturalness of unprinted paper, the subtlety of intelligent typography. An aesthetic of modesty and understated design will follow.

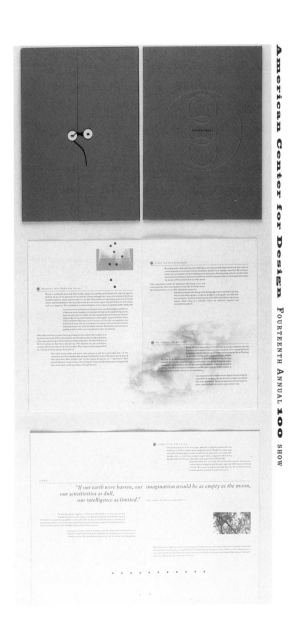

DESIGNERS

Michael Glass, Kerry Grady

WRITER

Bill McDowell

PHOTOGRAPHER

Francois Robert

DESIGN FIRM

Michael Glass Design, Inc.

CLIENT

RR Donnelley

TYPOGRAPHER

Typographic Resource

PRINTER

RR Donnelley

OBJECTIVES

Inform and educate

AUDIENCES

Internal, consumer

BM

It is a very nicely designed piece of work and a good effort in the right direction. But it's printed in six colors on the cover. It comes in a package the size of the cover, but is then placed in an envelope that is printed and embossed all the way through. It's certainly a beautifully designed publication. The question is: how do designers and printers deal with the problem with promoting environmental consciousness? It seems contradictory to me to print something to promote environmental awareness.

Product Liability in the United States

Part of the client's intention in publishing this book was to position the law firm as the authority in the area of product liability law. The book was published in both a hardcover and a paperback edition and was meant both to educate and attract new clients to the firm. The subject matter – when manufacturers are sued for injury attributed to their product – is actually fertile ground for illustration ideas, and David Johnson's drawings were central to enlivening the somewhat dry legal text of this book. Elegance, authority, and legibility were criteria for the book design. This client has always insisted on the highest caliber of design in its presentation materials, and for this we continue to thank them.

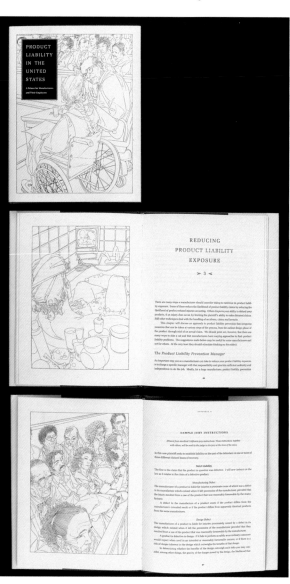

DESIGNERS
Ginny Perleins, Ellen Ziegler

ART DIRECTOR
Ellen Ziegler

WRITERS
Keith Gerrand, Tom McLaughlin

ILLUSTRATOR
David Johnson

DESIGN FIRM
Ellen Ziegler Design

CLIENT
Perkins Coie

TYPOGRAPHER
Bitstream

PRINTER
Impressions NW

PAPERS
Starwhite Vickssburg, ESSE

OBJECTIVES
Inform and educate

AUDIENCE
Corporate

BM

Their goal was to make a potentially dry book as interesting and legible as possible, and they've been 100 percent successful. It's a very clear presentation of the material with engaging illustrations that are unusual for this kind of material. The information is well organized and well ordered. The reader is able to enter the space of the book and find what they are looking for easily.

Lou Reed/John Cale: Songs for Drella
Retail CD Digipak

This was our attempt to create a fitting memorial to Andy Warhol while at the same time giving tribute to the seminal rock band Velvet Underground. Our choice of materials was obvious, as was the color scheme. Our hope was to create a package not only as homage to the principal players, but also to convey a historical sense of the time. The type had to remain simple and direct. Images were chosen through a natural process of elimination.

DESIGNERS

Tom Recchion, Sylvia Reed

WRITERS

John Cale, Lou Reed, Bill Bentley

DESIGN FIRM

Warner Bros. Records

CLIENT

Sire Records

PRINTER

Ivy Hill

SEPARATOR

Color Inc.

OBJECTIVE

Generate interest in recording artist

AUDIENCES

Radio and retail

American Center for Design FOURTEENTH ANNUAL 100 SHOW

BM

The beauty in this is that it's necrophilia without nostalgia.

It really is a luscious piece of work. It's hard to resist.

T-Shirt ADVERTISEMENT

ENTRANT'S COMMENTS

I tried to create an ad that would appeal to the particular audience of Beach Culture magazine. I felt a graphic treatment would be more effective than simply displaying the shirt, like most t-shirt ads. The goal was to communicate to the viewer that if they liked our magazine, then this was a t-shirt they might want in their wardrobe, sight-unseen.

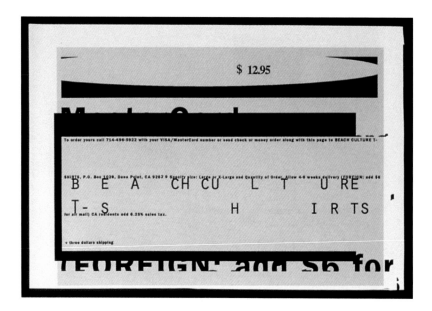

DESIGNER

David Carson

DESIGN FIRM

Carson Design

CLIENT

Beach Culture

TYPOGRAPHER

Carson

PRINTER

Maxwell

SEPARATOR

American

OBJECTIVE

Support of sales

AUDIENCE

Consumer

BM

What can you say about it; it's a great little ad. This has the inventiveness and quality of Beach Culture, which is hard to do on a such a modest scale.

Wexner Center NEWSLETTER

ENTRANT'S COMMENTS

Established as a multidisciplinary contemporary arts institution, The Wexner Center for the Arts offers progessive programming in the visual arts, film and video, performing arts and education. The center's newsletter is produced monthly, providing patrons and the general public with detailed information on all scheduled events in each of the four program areas. One of the primary and challenging objectives in the ongoing design of this publication is to reflect the vitality, diversity and risk-taking aspects of the center's programming. The opportunity to design within a series allows us to emphasize process rather than product, thereby reinforcing the Wexner Center's role as a laboratory for art. The publication continues to evolve and mature with the institution, growing into, out of and around the square grid – an obvious reference to the Wexner Center's immediately recognizable architechure.

DESIGNER

Gary Sankey

ART DIRECTOR

Oscar Fernandez

WRITER

Elizabeth Krouse

DESIGN FIRM

Wexner Center Design Dept.

CLIENT

Wexner Center for the Arts

TYPOGRAPHER

Harlan Type

PRINTERS

Robin Enterprises, Inc., Fine Line Graphics

PAPER

Hammermill Offset Opaque

OBJECTIVES

Generate inquiry, inform and educate

AUDIENCE

Consumer

BM

The system in this case is really smart. That's why I love it. There is a very strong grid in this series but the grid allows for a great deal of deviation within it. The way these things are spaced and handled varies from one issue to another while retaining a consistency, which is a hard thing to achieve without either falling on one side into chaos or on the other into boredom. On the inside they handle an enormous quantity of text. With only a small staff to produce such a large quantity of stuff, it's really pretty impressive.

ENTRANT'S COMMENTS

The posters and announcements hanging in CalArt's hallways have created fierce competition for the reader's attention, so I designed this poster with intrigue and clarity as primary objectives. I was also interested in how the information could be playfully consumed. From across the hall a "jiggly" blue shape in quotation marks, suggesting both a world and moving body parts, draws the viewer in. This image is a play on the word "world", the central design theme and a shortened nickname for the festival. The event titles, activated (dancing?) in a mono-spaced typeface, form phonetic combinations that create new related words. Since the poster is text heavy, I thought it would be read in successive readings so I grouped specific phrases together anticipating that the reader would walk away with only parts of the information. These groupings emphasize ideas that relate to the world theme or specific information, such as dates, times, and places. Everything is overprinted by a large yellow shape that unites the composition into a flag or banner.

DESIGNER
Caryn Aono

DESIGNFIRM
CalArts Public Affairs Office

CLIENT
CalArts

PRINTER
Samper Silkscreen

PAPER
Nekoosa vellum cover

OBJECTIVES
Generate inquiry, inform and educate

AUDIENCE
Music performance-going public

BM

Something that came up in the jurors' discussion was a desire to see pieces with clarity. This is one of the most beautiful and clear pieces in the show. It has a very simple image as an initial statement: a world in quotation marks. The way it is resolved spatially is superb. The way that the country, or in some cases the continent, is kept separate, as a noun instead of as an adjective, is very nice. It's very complex typography, but it's so well organized, so clearly functional, that the intervention doesn't disturb it. It adds to the layering.

Design
in Review

The
Year

BROADCAST CONTRACT DESIGN
INTERIOR DESIGN
INDUSTRIAL DESIGN
ENVIRONMENTAL GRAPHIC DESIGN

BROADCAST DESIGNERS
ASSOCIATION

James A. Houff

Chair

1991 Design Competition   James A. Houff is Design Director for
WDIV-TV of Detroit, Michigan, and
President of James A. Houff Design. He
served as co-chair of the 1991 BDA Seminar.

IN ORDER TO REVIEW THIS YEAR'S
Broadcast Designers Association (BDA) show I must simultaneously review the current state
of video technology. We are still inexorably tied to the tools we use to produce our work, which
is both a blessing and a curse. It is a blessing because our tools now offer us unlimited visual possibilities. It is a
curse because aspects of this relationship with technology have caused broadcast design to be overlooked by the
more established design community. I would note three reasons why our work is not taken seriously: 1) we have
been intoxicated with our own technological capabilities; 2) viewers have become numbed by the ubiquitous
nature of television and by extension numbed to our work; and 3) perhaps our print colleagues have had an
unspoken envy of our equipment and unprecedented exposure.

Video technology has advanced to the point that what the designer's mind can conceive, the tools can now
make happen, seamlessly and flawlessly. This seamless, flawless quality oils powerful design material, helping it
to slip past our eyes and off the roster of design disciplines. Our
work slides by in fleeting seconds, disappearing into the ether. It has
never been physically touched, walked into, sat on, or displayed on a re-
frigerator, let alone on a museum wall. However, the television set, the
messenger of this medium, sits in every home as benignly as a refrig-
erator and as powerfully as "Big Brother." There is a numbing synthesis
of "disposable distraction" and "voice from above" that abstracts the
images brought home to the viewer through the TV set. The images are
not made of human hands. They become disguised as something other
than us, either above us or below us, but certainly not of us. Think again.
Television has become the primary source of news, information and en-
tertainment in the United States with no end in sight for future proliferation and development. The pioneers of
the graphic design of the 21st century are the hands and minds behind this
overlooked disci- pline, called broadcast design.

Much of this pioneering can be likened to an adolescent phase.
The lightning speed of developments in video technology over the last
ten years has made practitioners in the field both dizzy and perhaps
bloated from overfeeding on technique. As new techniques presented
themselves either through hardware or software, the voracious appetite of
the hungry TV set ate up these effects as quickly as designers saw them, fell
in love with them, exploited them and regurgitated them in a predictable
round of follow the leader. Fads and trends are visible in any field;
broadcast design, however, has devoured its own advancements the minute
they arrived on the scene. We have over-glitzed ourselves, and have been too pleased with ourselves, too amazed
by our "toys." The result has been a tremendous
amount of work that exhibited effect for the sake of
effect. This often inappropriate dominance of "form
over substance" is largely responsible for our not
being taken seriously by the design world.

This "form over substance" tendency, I am
happy to report, seems to be fading for a couple of
reasons. First of all, the "toys" have been around for
a while. We have gotten over our new found abilities
to make anything and everything marble, gold or
chrome, and make it fly through space, just because
we can. Secondly, there has been a general leveling off of advancements, which now seem to be putting

Cabarestafette,
NOB Design,
Netherlands;
Geert van Ooijen,
designer; Will
Baker, art
director

HBO Fall Campaign ID, HBO New York; Joano Paulo Schlitler, Tama Goen, Lisa Lloyd, designers; Orest Woronewych, art director

more of the tools into more people's hands. This is due to the fact that technologies tend to miniaturize, condense and become more affordable over time. Hand in hand with the proliferation of the tools comes the demand for new and different looks in order to make one stand out in the marketplace. In other words, now that everyone can do chrome, what do you do? The new looks seem to be coming from blending different video sources, looks that previously had been experienced in a purer, more singular form when the technique was still new on the scene. This type of work has been termed "blendo," and this year's BDA show indicates the current preference for this approach.

Some of this has been seen in recent BDA shows over the past few years, and there are admirable examples of it in this year's show. But more risks can be taken to achieve a more appropriate and intrinsic relationship between promotion, packaging and the audience. It is here that design can begin to take a front row seat in the "media-industrial" complex. Using rap music to sell McDonalds to a black audience is not an ideal use of this concept. A better example might be promos for HA! (a comedy channel) that would present facts regarding the AIDS crisis as part of a campaign called "Not A Laughing Matter."

This year's BDA show is testimony to the fact that television is a mirror of our culture. As minorities and their multiplicity of voices become more audible in society, so are programming outlets and their accompanying identities which are shaped by broadcast designers. But has video technology's ability to diversify and expand spurred on our coverage, catering to and accepting of diversity? Or has society's diversification created the need, to which technology has in turn responded? I suspect, sadly, that technology, rather than a cited need, led the way toward this embrace of diversity. It has been enlightened and perhaps opportunistic individuals, however, who have learned how to put it to good use. I do not miss the days when "Leave it to Beaver" was the only portrayal of life in America available for television consumption. Likewise, happily, all typography on television is no longer restricted to flying plastic or chrome.

Recently the Museum of Television and Radio opened in Manhattan. It is New York's first new major museum in twenty-five years. Randall Rothenberg of *The New York Times* asks, "Is the collection merely an artifact of recent history, or does it contain modern art? Is the museum an academy of enlightened cultural understanding, or a temple of kitsch? Are television and radio, though undeniably shapers of society, worthy of a museum's ennoblement, or should they be condemned as corrupters of literacy?" In the same article Rothenberg quotes Adam Gopnik, staff writer at the *New Yorker* and the co-curator of the recent exhibit "High and Low" at the Museum of Modern Art. That exhibit attempted, according to Rothenberg, to "curatorially and intellectually dismantle the barriers placed between categories of culture." Gopnik says that television must be also analyzed as art in terms of its craftsmanship, technique, intent and meaning. "We live in a fallen world where good and bad and venal and noble impulses are hopelessly mixed," Mr. Gopnik said. "When you say, 'Because something is on commercial television it cannot be interesting,' you are applying dogma, not judgement."

Where does such debate place broadcast design? As co-chair of the 1991 BDA seminar that took place in Baltimore, I was able to invite many people from outside the immediate realm of broadcast design to speak to our members. One guest, Michael Vanderbyl, stated that "TV has inherited the culture. It has an accessibility to art that touches everyday life." He also stated that as "public artists" we have a "social responsibility to express our passion, humor and love for what we do and find expression through commercial art." Michael's comments point to a current debate: Is graphic design the transparent vehicle of another's message? Or is there room for the designer to insert expression? This issue has been colorfully brought to the forefront through the controversial and expressive work presented in the recent book, *Cranbrook Design: The New Discourse.* Perhaps I am prejudiced, being an alumnus of Cranbrook, but like Michael, I too feel there is room for designers to assert expression and meaning into their work. Nowhere are designers being asked to take a more visible role than are broadcast designers in shaping packaging for television. If graphic designers want to take a front seat in the media-industrial complex, broadcast design will perhaps make that possible. It is up to us. This year's BDA show bears witness to the fact that we are already up and running – with our most exciting and meaningful work hopefully yet in front of us.

Spring/Summer BBC2, British Broadcasting Corporation; Brendon Norman-Ross, Jane Wyatt, Mark Chaudoir, designers

Charles D. Gandy

Charles D. Gandy is President of Gandy/
Peace, Inc., an Atlanta-based interior
design firm. He is a Fellow of the American
Society of Interior Designers and an
Honorary Member of the Interior Design
Educator's Council.

INTERIOR DESIGN. WHAT IS IT? WHERE is it? Where has it been? Where is it going? Just what is this thing we call "interior design"?

These basic questions are omnipresent in any profession, but asking them at this time seems extremely appropriate for interior design, for we are at a crucial turning point in our profession. We are coming into our own, we are growing up, we are maturing, we are moving into the last decade of this century, and preparing for the next. Making such a broad statement may seem rather obvious, even trite; after all every profession is making plans for the future. But for interior design it is more than a "journalistic" statement. It is true. For finally, after several decades of uncertainty, even confusion, the profession of interior design is coming into its own. Designers, as a group, have realized our importance in the overall health, safety, and welfare issues of today's society. We are actively contributing to the overall team of professionals responsible for the built environment. Working in close collaboration with other designers, architects, and engineers, we are creating interior spaces that are responding to the needs of our well-informed and demanding clients. The results are dramatic and exciting.

The recent IBD/Interior Design Magazine contract design competition serves as an excellent barometer of the status of the profession by providing a microcosm of what is and is not happening in the actual practice of interior design. The parameters of the competition were simple: entrants could submit any contract interior including but not limited to retail, hospitality, dining facilities, corporate offices, renovation, and institutional or cultural facilities. The work could not have been published previously and had to have been completed within the last two years. Two days of meticulous viewing of hundreds of photographs of installations produced ten winners with one of those being selected as the best overall of the competition. With spaces in all the above mentioned categories submitted, the entrants ran the gamut. Unsurprisingly, the interiors of corporate offices outnumbered the other categories combined.

The quality and variety of the entries in the corporate office category underscored today's business community's understanding of the value of good design. Whether this is a question of creating and/or projecting a certain image, improving productivity and morale, or, hopefully, a combination of both of these goals, the corporate interiors being designed today reflect a common thread of quality and solidity. An awareness of today's troubled economic times would suggest that corporate America's interiors are smaller and less glamorous than similar spaces of the previous decade. Indeed, there were some examples – both good and better – of smaller, more pragmatic spaces. But as a whole, there was a richness and grandness that more than emulated the go-for-broke approach of the 1980s. This was not an arrogant display of opulence for its own sake, but instead a solid sense of control over moderate to expensive budgets with an eye to the long-term benefits justifying such expenditures. In many cases the interiors submitted were reworks of previous spaces. Some were for adaptive use of existing buildings. Many had programs that required multipurpose functions. Two such winners summarize the entire field.

*Klein Tools Inc.,
Gensler and
Associates/
Architects*

Recognized by the jury as the best of the competition, a showroom, conference, and training facility designed by the Los Angeles office of Gensler and Associates/Architects for Klein Tools, Inc., incorporated many traits typical of today's corporate interior. By carefully adapting an existing structure to showcase an archival collection of the company's products (tools) the design team capitalized on an appropriate use of "high-tech" industrial materials, built-in flexibility, dramatic lighting, and strong

architectural forms to emphasize the company's image in a successful and exciting space. The presentation/ conference room for Kraft Foodservice in Deerfield, Illinois, designed by The Environments Group of Chicago, dramatically succeeded in providing an inviting multipurpose space with a sense of humor. The plan featured a

curved wall and soffit and a rich palate of materials including wooden and lacquered panels and fabric covered walls, as well as a host of options regarding lighting and furniture arrangement. The built-in flexibility meets the constant agenda changes required by the client.

These two winners gained the attention of the jury because they embodied a challenging plan, finish, or overall solution. While it is exciting that the corporate interior has come into its own, it is less than exciting that an almost uniform corporate look has emerged. Regionalism and individualism have given way to conformity, albeit quality conformity.

Corporate America is not alone in recognizing the benefits of good design. The retail community demonstrated its awareness that good design sells. One stellar installation was for Final Call!, the large discount center of Nieman Marcus. The vast spaces of this warehouse liquidating facility were designed to compel discount shopping while simultaneously maintaining the high-end image of the store. Playful yet stylish vignettes for quantity selling of quality goods at discount prices made inspired use of simple and inexpensive building materials in exciting shapes and colors, highlighted by dramatic lighting.

The work of this year's designers also underscores another recent area of concentration, socially responsible design. A number of projects were submitted for long-term care homes, child day-care centers, and nursing/ hospital centers, executed with appropriate care and attention to detail. In some cases the end result may not have been as "pretty" as other more glamorous spaces, but without question, the function of these spaces was emphasized. The use of ergonomic seating with appropriate chair bases and good arm supports, proper lighting

incorporating higher foot candles than "normal," and strong vivid color with good contrasts, made the spaces work on one level. The lack of aesthetic appeal, to a design jury, meant that none of these spaces was cited as being a "winner." Long laborious discussions did and should result about the responsibility of the design community – designers and manufacturers alike – to meet the needs of this specialized and growing population in a manner that not only meets their functional requirements but also stimulates and heightens their emotional and aesthetic sensitivities. Also there was an unusually large number of installations of religious facilities which, like the corporate offices, displayed a rich, varied and inspired palate of shape, form, and material based on traditional iconography.

Without question, the IBD/Interior Design Magazine competition proved that there is a lot of work being done, most of it good. Unfortunately, like other design professionals, many interior designers are imitators and not innovators. More often than not, today's spaces mimic other spaces. Thankfully, most chose good role models to emulate. This lack of innovation may indeed result from the expectations of the client, who too often demands what has been before. Nonetheless, it is imperative that as our profession continues to grow and mature, we concentrate on creativity, on research, and on continually raising the level of design to a higher plane. Even with this somewhat less than positive commentary, the interior design profession is alive and well and looking forward to making even greater strides as we move into the next century.

Kraft Foodservice Presentation Room, The Environments Group

Neiman Marcus Last Call, Hermanovski Lauck Design

Gerald P. Hirshberg

As Vice President of Nissan Design International, Inc., Jerry Hirshberg has been responsible for internationalizing the design thinking of Nissan Motor Co., Ltd. NDI designs products ranging from automobiles to medical instruments to vacuum cleaners, reflecting Jerry's belief that diversity leads to creativity.

"**H**OW WAS THE PARTY LAST night?" is a question that has always left me somewhat confused. Does the answer depend on the number of worthwhile people I met? Or is it the quality of the food and music? Or is it the level of noise, the length of time it lasted, or the level of sobriety (or the lack of it) that determines the answer?

This same confusion surrounds the judging of a museum show. How many works of art is it necessary to be "blown away" by to feel that the show is worthwhile? (In a national survey of museum directors a few years ago, most directors said one or two!) Is it the overall quality of the pieces in the show or the nature and number of exceptional

pieces? Or is it the strength and audacity of the organizing theme?

I raise these issues, having been asked to comment on the current state of the product design profession and to make observations gleaned from my experience as chairperson of the jury for the 1991 IDEA Awards Program. As with the party and museum show, I find myself wondering how to assess this experience. Are the top award winners the key indicators of the health of the profession and do they point in the direction of its trajectory? Is the design quality of the winners or their sheer number more revealing? Or is it the totality of all the submissions as a group that constitutes the clearest viewpoint? After all, each entry was considered exceptional by the designer who created it and thus should surely provide a perspective on the profession's current view of itself. And isn't that more significant a judgement than that of a handful of jurors? There are no easy answers to these questions.

The assumption is that a design competition reflects something about the profession and the world. Design itself is surely a mirror of both the professional and societal cultures from which it emerges. In an open competition such as the IDEA Awards Program where individuals select their own best work to submit, it is certainly a form of professional self-assessment.

One clear message emerged from the contrast between exploratory and production design. Since conceptual products were categorized separately from those products that found their way into mass production, it was immediately evident that the quality of the concept work was often significantly more spirited, pure and appropriate to today's markets than much of the production work. Tandem's Concept 2000 Computer System and Digital Equipment Corporation's Large Screen LCD Video Projector, as well as the amazing Bungieboarding-Bungie, were refreshing and bold statements.

Large Screen LCD Video Projector, Digital Equipment Corporation; Meg Hetfield, designer

Perhaps the contrast between concept and production design was most dramatically seen in the automotive industry. If highly feasible concept vehicles such as the Dodge Neon or Ford Contour are being generated from the design and engineering departments, why are they, or vehicles with comparable freshness, not finding their way to the road? Something is happening between concept and production that is sapping the energy and freshness of the designs. That grey area can only be attributed to the army of "professional second-guessers" populated by traditional marketers, planners and assorted executives.

The automobile business is one of the most dramatic examples of this widespread and old problem. The higher the level of investment in a product, the higher the level of second-guessing. Whenever risk is involved there is a tendency to turn away from intuition and creative design toward the illusory comfort

of numbers and "rational thinking." The only certain result of this kind of risk avoidance are products that look designed to avoid risk, surely a dubious (and risky) corporate message. The competition provided a graphic glimpse at this phenomenon.

Another undeniable observation concerned the overall strength of professional equipment design compared to that for the general consumer market. Categories including medical instrumentation, computer hardware, industrial and business equipment and other specialized products were far more imposing than automobiles, furniture, housewares and appliances. It is unsettling to see a delightfully audacious, witty yet rugged computer such as The Brick next to a tame, derivative collection of chairs, lamps and televisions.

A competition can't tell you why such a thing is so - it can only make it an evident, visible phenomenon. When production costs are high and investment risks are escalated, we seem to fall back on safe ground. Indeed, there was so much re-hashing of trendy design cliches (i.e. wavy surfaces, fake concrete blocks, turquoise and salmon knobs set in diagonal recesses, Michael Graves' little squares, etc.) that one juror, Arnold Wasserman, proclaimed the need for a "design police." The idea was roundly applauded. Surely the need to follow trends is inversely proportional to real corporate and designer confidence.

Design paints a portrait of the corporate and societal cultures from which it emerges. Given the current level of ferment and growing recognition of the design profession, I was expecting a design "face" to emerge from the competition brimming with typical American exuberance and confidence. There have been significant articles about design in magazines from *Fortune* to *Time*, and considerable coverage in newspapers from *The New York Times* to *The Wall Street Journal*. *Business Week* elected to sponsor the IDEA Awards for the first time this year and will dedicate one issue annually to a discussion of the competition. Major universities such as Stanford, Carnegie Mellon and Harvard are exposing business and engineering departments to the principles of design. Departments of design are sprouting up in corporations that previously relegated it to low level priority. And there have been countless conferences where the central theme has been the critical role that design is finally being seen to play in our international competitiveness.

JuiceMate, California State University; Bart André, designer; Michael Kammermeyer, advisor

Concept 2000 Computer System, Tandem Computers Inc.; John Guenther, Brett Lovelady, designers

Yet with all this acknowledgement, design does not seem to be responding with confidence. The most recent conference themes and articles center around questions of whether we are ready for the spotlight, and whether we can deliver on what we've been promising. Perhaps the tentative, toned-down quality of so much of our design is mirroring something deeper about the current mood of the country rather than any recognition of the profession itself. It would appear that design is more responsive to deep cultural stirrings and shifts than to professional issues. Perhaps this is both appropriate and useful. Design serves on one level as a continuously changing monitor of our tastes, moods and priorities.

Tadpole Infant Positioning System, Tumble Forms Inc.; Michael Gravel, Kristine Wohnsen, designers

But design is not solely reactive. It can also generate fresh cultural directions and regenerate latent energies. The best designs in the competition are vivid, brashly original, and often brilliant, and many display a growing sensitivity and responsiveness to emerging concerns with human issues. Product award winners such as the Drake Willock System 1000 Dialysis Machine, the Animal Wet Suit, the Juice Mate, the Encore Portable Heaters, and the Tadpole Physically Impaired Infant Exercise System, all exemplify these qualities.

My hope and belief is that the current cultural hesitancy we are experiencing will turn into a mature thoughtfulness and depth of design. While the atmosphere remains somewhat cloudy as we near the end of the century, one senses that the party is not yet over.

Virginia Gehshan

Virginia Gehshan is a partner in Cloud and Gehshan Associates, Inc., a graphic design firm in Philadelphia. Her firm creates architectural signage, identity programs and marketing communications for a diverse group of clients. She is a founding member of the SEGD Philadelphia chapter and a member of the SEGD Education Committee.

ENVIRONMENTAL GRAPHIC design is easily the most ubiquitous form of design in our culture. Whether we are in pristine farm country, on a secluded footpath in a national park, or in the dense urban/suburban landscape, we are rarely beyond the reach of signs. But only a fraction of them are "designed."

Environmental graphic design embraces more than sign design, claiming the broader territory of "built" communications, both verbal and non-verbal. This year's competition entries included exhibits, waterfalls, showrooms, flags, bird houses and lighting, in addition to the more conventional sign programs. In a profession that includes graphic designers, architects and industrial designers as its three largest constituents, this eclectic mix of projects is the norm.

Though its history is brief, practitioners of environmental graphic design are confronted with an unusual variety of challenges in their everyday design process: increasingly restrictive sign codes and public officials that attempt to regulate "bad signs", but instead reduce design opportunity; legislative bombshells such as the Americans with Disability Act which threaten to remove any individuality from signs designed for the public; a sign program's growing need for changeability and vandal resistance; producing fine typography with computerized sign making equipment; architects who "would do it themselves if they had the time," or architects who acknowledge the need for signs but don't want them in evidence on their buildings; clients who have not purchased signs or graphic design services before and cannot believe their cost; and the need to keep learning and educating everyone else about this young profession.

In the context of these obstacles, were this year's judges at all forgiving? No. They were critical, vigorous and decisive in their selections. The result of their deliberations was a series of clear opinions about design practices and priorities:

Distill the idea. The judges wanted projects to be simple, strong and dramatic. They were looking for entries that expressed a single idea with confidence and economy. Many of the award-winning designs have an almost Spartan quality – direct, singular in purpose, eloquent.

Transcend the program. It was generally assumed that the projects submitted reflected the program of the client. If the program was judged trivial, wasteful or just plain mundane, the designer's work became guilty by association. Malls? Fast food chains? Company shrines? This is where retail and corporate entries suffered. The judges saw much of the work as inappropriate, overdone or formulaic. Are the client and the program as much the object of criticism as the designer? Was the negative reaction a simple disdain for big business? "Not so," said the judges. "This work is lousy no matter who it is for." The implication here, though, is that each designer can and

Reston Town Center, Reston, Virginia; Reston Town Center Associates, Himmel/MKDG & Mobil Land Development; RTKL Associates Inc., designers; George Pillorge, principal

*Commemorative
Art and Inscription
Installation*,
Jefferson High
Schoool, Los
Angeles, California;
BJ Krivanek Art
and Design,
designers; BJ
Krivanek, principal

should move beyond the client's directive, beyond conventional wisdom and industry formulas, and solve the problem at hand with greater ingenuity.

Break new ground. The jurors wanted innovation. One juror described health care projects as looking like ten year old corporate work. There were comments like "nothing new," or "I've seen that before."

Let's examine this desire for innovation. Products resulting from the American obsession with what is "new" clog our landfills. The unending desire for "new" and "fresh" is very much a part of our culture, and one that most designers have participated in wholeheartedly. But there was a visionary motive to this jury's quest for innovative ideas. What emerged in the post-judging analysis were more rigorous criteria for what is both truly innovative and socially enlightened, including:

Plurality. Projects that reflect the diversity of the client and context. Expressing a client's identity in a way that is more complex and less monolithic. *Pioneering.* Rejecting design and industry formulas so that projects of the same type do not all look alike; unpredictable. *Humanity.* Projects that reflect a multiplicity of users. Solutions which are influenced by music, art, dance and mixed media. Ideas with humor, heart and soul. *Modularity.* Projects that allow reconfiguration and reuse of their component parts, especially in areas of frequent change, such as showrooms. *Sensitivity to context.* Projects that relate to where they are, and respond directly to the climate, culture, people and landscape. A rejection of artificial environments. Sign programs with visual sequencing that relate appropriately to the environment. *Less is more.* The modernist creed in an ecological context. Projects that use less material and reveal a stronger idea, or that minimize the proliferation of signs in the environment. Solutions that pose a meaningful response to a world of increasing scarcity.

Like the designs they espoused, the directives of the jury were passionate and blunt. Their conclusions, in a nutshell, read like rules for living: make it honest, cut away the frills, think for yourself, give it feeling, pursue excellence. These are principles to which we can all aspire.

*Taft Museum
Promotional
Exhibit*,
Westin Hotel
Lobby-Atrium,
Cincinnatti, Ohio;
Graphic Design
Class, University
of Cincinnatti,
designers;
Robert Prost,
Nick Chaparos,
Professors

Design Offices
Represented

Adobe Systems Inc.
1585 Charleston Rd.
Mountain View, CA 94043

Alexander Isley Design
361 Broadway, Suite 111
New York, NY 10013

Alfred A. Knopf, Inc.
201 E. 50th St., 7th Floor
New York, NY 10022

Allen Hori
PO Box 25058
3001 HB Rotterdam
The Netherlands

Amy Srubas/Michael Giammanco
3323 N. Paulina #5C
Chicago, IL 60657

Andrew Blauvelt
1021 Wirewood Dr. #301
Raleigh, NC 27605

Art Center College of Design
1700 Lida St.
Pasadena, CA 91103

Art Chantry Design
PO Box 4069
Seattle, WA 98104

Art Gallery of Ontario
317 Dundas St. W.
Toronto, Ontario M5T 1G4

Barry Deck Design
1048 N. Marshfield
Chicago, IL 60622

Barsuhn Design
420 N. Fifth St., Suite 1086
Minneapolis, MN 55401

California Institute for the Arts
24700 McBean Parkway
Valencia, CA 91355

Carson Design
128-1/2 Tenth St.
Del Mar, CA 92104

Chermayeff & Geismar Inc.
15 E. 26th St., 12th Floor
New York, NY 10010

Commbine
1605 W. 31st St.
Minneapolis, MN 55408

Crocker, Inc.
210 Lincoln St., Suite 405
Boston, MA 02111

Cross Associates
3465 W. 6th St., Suite 300
Los Angeles, CA 90020

Dayton Hudson Marshall Field's
700 Nicollet Mall
Minneapolis, MN 55402

Design Provisions
190 Grand St.
New York, NY 10013

Earl Gee Design
501 Second St., Suite 700
San Francisco, CA 94107

Ellen Ziegler Design
114 W. Denny Way, Suite 250
Seattle, WA 98119

Fitch RichardsonSmith
PO Box 360
Worthington, OH 43085

Frankfurt Gips Balkind
244 E. 58th St.
New York, NY 10022

Gottschalk + Ash International
2050 Mansfield, Suite 900
Montréal, Québec H3A 1Y9

Group C
109 Livingston St.
New Haven, CT 06511

Hallmark Cards, Inc.
2501 McGee Mail Drop 266
Kansas City, MO 64111

Heavy Meta
116 W. 29th St. #9W
New York, NY 10001

Herb Lubalin Study Center
The Cooper Union
7 E. 7th St.
New York, NY 10003

J. Gibson and Co.
1320 19th St. NW, Suite 200
Washington, DC 20036

James A. Houff Design
392 St. Clair
Grosse Pointe, MI 48230

Jessica Shatan
144 Seventh Ave.
Brooklyn, NY 11215

Joani Spadaro
1315 Lutz Ave.
Raleigh, NC 27607

Kerr and Company
201-1102 Homer St.
Vancouver, BC V6B 2X6

Lausten/Cossutta Design
5820 Wilshire Blvd., Suite 601
Los Angeles, CA 90036

M Plus M Incorporated
17 Cornelia St.
New York, NY 10014

M&Co.
50 W. 17th St., 12th Floor
New York, NY 10011

Margaret Morton
101 E. 15th St., 3rd Floor
New York, NY 10003

Mark Oldach Design
2138 W. Haddon Ave.
Chicago, IL 60622

Michael Glass Design
213 W. Institute Place, Suite 608
Chicago, IL 60610

Mr. Keedy
574 S. Ogden Dr.
Los Angeles, CA 90036

Museum of Contemporary Art
237 E. Ontario
Chicago, IL 60611

One Good Dog
807 Woodcrest Dr.
Royal Oak, MI 48067

Ostro Design
147 Fern St.
Hartford, CT 06105

Pentagram
212 Fifth Avenue
New York, NY 10010

Peterson & Company
2200 N. Lamar
Dallas, TX 75202

Ph.D
1616 Ocean Park Blvd.
Santa Monica, CA 90405

plus design inc.
10 Thatcher St., Suite 109
Boston, MA 02113

R Sirko Design
621 Fox Point Dr.
Chesterton, IN 46304

Rebecca Chamlee Design
2545 W. 5th St.
Los Angeles, CA 90057

Richardson or Richardson
1301 E. Bethany Home Rd.
Phoenix, AZ 85014

Ron Kellum Design
1133 Broadway, Rm. 1214
New York, NY 10010

Rosenworld
45 Lispenard Street
New York, NY 10013

Sametz Blackstone Associates
40 W. Newton St.
Boston, MA 02118

Schmeltz + Warren
74 Sheffield Rd.
Columbus, OH 43214-2541

Skolos/Wedell
529 Main St.
Charlestown, MA 02129

Smart Design, Inc.
7 W. 18th St., 8th Floor
New York, NY 10011

Studio Dumbar
Kanaalweg 34C
2584 CK Den Haag
The Netherlands

Sussman/Prejza & Co., Inc.
3960 Ince Blvd.
Culver City, CA 90232

Tenazas Design
605 Third St., Suite 208
San Francisco, CA 94107

The Post Press
16 Thompson Lane
Newark, DE 19711

Thirst
855 W. Blackhawk
Chicago, IL 60622

Thomas Starr & Associates
23 E. 37th St.
New York, NY 10016

Tolleson Design
444 Spear St., Suite 204
San Francisco, CA 94105

University of Texas at Austin
502 E. 42nd St.
Austin, TX 78751

Warner Bros. Records
3300 Warner Blvd.
Burbank, CA 91505

Wexner Center for the Arts
N. High St. at 15th Ave.
Columbus, OH 43210

x height
4434 Matilija Ave.
Sherman Oaks, CA 91423

Zender + Associates, Inc.
2311 Park Ave.
Cincinnati, OH 45206